Deliverance from the Down Low

Deliverance from the Down Low

Deliverance For Men Who Sleep With Men But Profess To Be Straight

G.L. Williams

ACW Press
Ozark, AL 36360

Deliverance from the Down Low
Copyright ©2005 G.L. Williams
All rights reserved

Cover Design by Bryant Design
Interior Design by Pine Hill Graphics

Packaged by ACW Press
1200 HWY 231 South #273
Ozark, AL 36360
www.acwpress.com
The views expressed or implied in this work do not necessarily reflect those of ACW Press. Ultimate design, content, and editorial accuracy of this work is the responsibility of the author(s).

Library of Congress Cataloging-in-Publication Data
(Provided by Cassidy Cataloguing Services, Inc.)

Williams, G.L.

    Deliverance from the down low : deliverance for men who sleep with men but profess to be straight / G.L. Williams. -- 1st ed. -- Ozark, AL : ACW Press, 2005.

      p. ; cm.
      ISBN: 1-932124-59-4

      1. African American bisexual men--United States. 2. Bisexual men--United States. 3. Homosexuality--Religious aspects. 4. Bisexuality--Religious aspects. 5. Bisexuality in marriage. I. Title.

BL65.H64 W55 2005
200/.86/642--dc22   0505

Printed in the United States of America.

Acknowledgements

To Christ, my Savior, for giving me both the insight and illumination to transfer my thoughts into print; it is through your Spirit that I live, move, and have my being.

To Maxine my queenly wife, thank you for your unfeigned love, your loyal support, and your faith to follow me as I follow the Lord. You are my friend, my baker, my sweet potato pie maker.

To Steve and Earnest, you are more than co-laborers and employees, you are my friends. Both of you have ministered to me in so many ways you will never know—thanks.

To my "agent" Sonja, thanks for all your hard work. I know that interacting with me was probably harder than reading this material.

To my gang, "Kei, Kei," "Jake," "Brit," and "Gdub," you guys are the greatest.

To my mother, who never wavered in your love and support of me.

To my big brother, Kenny, thanks for your prayers and words of encouragement.

To My uncle, thanks for sharing the wisdom of Solomon.

To Perry Mason, T.I. you are the bomb!

To my good friend "Burr Rabbit" (Elwyn).
Thanks for all of your prayers.

Special thanks to my "war buddy" (Sampson).
Keep hope alive!

To all of those who comprise the "First Church," you are not just the church where the *"Word is Changing Lives,"* you are the church that changed my life.

To the late Rev. Dr. R. T. Williams (Pop!), you made me the man I am today. Pop, how could I ever repay you for your sermons, instructions, scolding, directions, and philosophy? One of my aims in life was to make you and Mom proud of me. I pray that I have.

Foreword

Before I became an actor, I was trained as a "Human Relations Specialist." When there were problems in schools or companies with racism, sexism or sexuality issues they'd call us to help find resolve. Sexuality issues were often more challenging to resolve than racial tensions. Often homosexuals felt as if they didn't fit anywhere. They weren't accepted in their families, churches or job sites. They were rejected even in their own races. This book is a refreshing read! To hear a "Man of God" say to a DL Brotha the same that he would say to a liar, fornicator, cheater or thief...*God loves you and God has a place for you, but living a lie ain't that place!*

Dr. Williams gives hope to that DL Brotha who believes his situation is helpless and hopeless. Dr. Williams uses divine wisdom instead of hypocritical judgments as he encourages the DL Brotha to stop hiding from God's purpose of his life, the same way that he hides his lifestyle from his wife and girlfriend. He ministers to the DL Brotha by sharing God's promise, if he discontinues rationalizing and procrastinating about surrendering to God's will, and comes before the All Mighty God with obedience and a willing mind and expectations to be delivered, our Lord is mighty enough to bring him out of his darkness into God's marvelous light!

So often I believe ministers make the terrible mistake of bashing and judging brothers who are straddling the fence, which pushes the DL Brothas into the arms of practicing homosexuals. The only "word" that many preachers administer to these brothers is a "word" of bitter gay bashings and criticisms, instead of tangible solutions to their tangible problems. Dr. Williams skillfully delves below the surface, and speaks deliverance and hope to the DL Brotha who has surrendered to a life of hopelessness.

Dr. Williams allows the DL Brotha to see that there is help for his undercover lifestyle. I encourage all brothers (and sisters) to read this powerful book! Dr. Williams informs the DL Brotha that he is not "helpless," for he can look to the hills which cometh his help, his help cometh from the Lord!

Tommy Ford
Actor & CEO/President of Model T. Ford Entertainment

Contents

Introduction

June 29, 2004 was a day that commenced both normal and routine. Although the day started routinely, it did not end that way. Having two appointments scheduled, I considered the day relatively normal. It was not until I met with my last scheduled appointment that my day was abruptly altered. After discussing the issues that were at hand, the couple I was meeting with asked me if I had ever heard about *"brothers on the down low."* Up until this point in my life, I had somewhat inwardly prided myself on having the ability to stay current with the issues of the day.

As the couple continued to educate me about Down Low brothers, I experienced the deer-in-the-headlights look. For me, this was something new under the sun. Bisexuality has been around for years, but never in my wildest dreams or nightmares did I ever think this was going on at such an alarming rate among African-American men.

As we continued to discuss the topic, the couple presented me with the May 3, 2004 edition of *Jet Magazine.* The featured story was about an African-American man who was married, with children, but was involved in intimate relationships with men. This was the Down Low. As I read the article, J.L. King, the featured person, stated that ministers, police officers, and even thugs on the street are living out this lifestyle. Surprisingly, the profession disparity is as wide as the age disparity. DL men range from 18 to 78. Although this was a shocking revelation, a bigger bombshell would follow.

King went on to state that a staggering 75 percent of black women who have contracted AIDS, contracted it from heterosexual sex. In other words, DL men are playing a pivotal role in infecting black women. According to King, "On the Down Low" became popular in songs like TLC's 1994 "Creep," and Brian McKnight's 1995 tune, "On the Down Low."[1]

My inspiration for writing this book is that I am mad as hell! I know that some of you who just read the last sentence would place more emphasis on what I just wrote as opposed to the pandemic travesty that is reaping spiritual and sexual genocide in our country. The Bible informs us that we have a right to be angry about certain things just as long as they do not cause us to sin. Since this nefarious lifestyle is touching our homes, schools, playgrounds, and especially our churches, it's time to get mad.

What should we be mad about? Mad about the fact that the moral fibers of our country are ripping apart at the seams. Mad at the fact that America the beautiful is sprinting down a path of no return. Rome of yesteryear crumbled within before it crumbled without. A contemporized America is following the same lead of a failed republic.

Those who love this country and the Judeo Christian beliefs it was founded upon, must wake up and become angry. As we awake out of our slumber, we must not awake to chaos but rather to a cause. Our anger must not be a hot anger but rather a cold one. Hot anger is anger that is uncontrolled, unfunneled, and unfocused. Cold anger is just the opposite. It is fueled by a cause, directed to a target, and focused on its objective.

On the night of June 29, 2004, I called a family conference to discuss J.L. King's article along with the Bible. Before having my oldest daughter to read the article aloud to her siblings, I had each child at the table read a passage of Scripture from

Romans chapter 1 commencing at verse 18. After they read a verse, I gave a simple interpretation of each verse. I wanted to make sure that my family understood that despite the tragic trends that are holding America hostage, the Word of God has and is the answer to life's perplexing problems.

The reason I am mad as hell is that Satan has upped the ante. We live in a world where there are no more boundaries. Right is now wrong and wrong is now right. Bad is good and good is bad. The parameters of life are no longer permanent but now they are erasable. Bisexuality is en vogue. Marital infidelity has become the norm and is no longer a misnomer. To be homosexual is to be normal and to be heterosexual is to be abnormal.

The moral fibers of this country are no longer coming apart in strands—they are now coming apart in swatches. Old-fashioned absolutes are out, while the go with the flow mentality is in. When will it all stop? When will it all end? When will it turn around?

Can things ever be as they were? As long as we remain like we are, the promise to our posterity will be an abyss of sensual immorality.

When I shut up heaven and there is no rain, or command the locusts to devour the land, or send pestilence among My people, if My people who are called by My name will humble themselves, and pray and seek My face, and turn from their wicked ways, then I will hear from heaven, and will forgive their sin and heal their land (2 Chronicles 7:13,14).

chapter
ONE

Dominion Gone Bad

So What's Up with the Down Low?

The intent of this book is to help to guide men who are struggling with their sexuality to understand both the role and the purpose for which they have been created. Since all men are created in the image and after the likeness of God, it is imperative that we find out what God expects of us. Any man who does not know what is expected of him by the Almighty will never be able to conform to the image or person by which God made him.

When a man is oblivious to the purpose for which he was created, his plight becomes difficult. In addition, he runs the risk of becoming what society wants him to be, or what he chooses. One should keep in mind that decisions determine destinies, and destinies are the results of decisions. What you decide to do today has an impact on where you will be tomorrow; and where you are tomorrow will be a result of the decision you make today. It is my prayer that this book will reveal to some and reaffirm to others the intent, purpose, and the essence for which man was created.

Rick Warren, in his book, *A Purpose Driven Life*, makes a very powerful and profound statement in the very first chapter. Contrary to what many popular books, seminars, and movies tell you, you will not discover the purpose of your life by looking within yourself.[2]

Maybe you have never thought about this, but there is no invention on earth that can convey to you what its purpose is. In order to discover the purpose of the invention, one must ask the inventor. For only the creator or the owner's manual can tell you what the purpose of the invention is.

We live in perilous times whereby people are creating different rules to an old game. Although life is tough, some things have always been relatively simple. There was a time when "boy could not wait to meet girl and girl could not wait to meet boy." Whatever happened to the guy that couldn't wait to go on a date with his honey? Whatever happened to men and women who would get married and have children together? Whatever happened to men who would work hard just to make sure that the wife and the babies had sufficient substance? Whatever happened to parents who had a desire to see their children excel beyond their own horizons? The reason America is exponentially changing for the worst is that everyone is making up his own rules as far as his or her own life is concerned.

Authority is something that you and I cannot elude. Authority is found in our homes, in our schools, and on our jobs. Everywhere we turn, there is authority. Authority suppresses and keeps the lid shut on a caldron of anarchy. In life, there are crew chiefs, team leaders, managers, supervisors, regional mangers, district mangers, presidents, CEOs, and the list can go on endlessly.

Why are these people of authority present in our lives? They are there because if they were not, this country would experience anarchy from sea to shining sea. Guess how many people would show up to work on time if they knew they would not be reprimanded or terminated? The numbers, no doubt, would be staggering. The right authority keeps us within the boundaries. The right authority keeps us honest. The right authority keeps us accountable. The right authority extracts the best out of us.

However, in stark contrast, wrong authority breeds dishonesty. The wrong authority gives you a permission slip to walk the halls of life as long as you desire. The wrong authority will make you accountable to no one other than your own opinions and notions. The reason a man has more liberty under wrong authority as opposed to right authority is that wrong authority is actually no authority at all.

Wrong authority gives you the right to change the rules if you do not like them. Wrong authority allows you to believe what you want to believe, feel how you want to feel, do what you want to do, and say what you want to say. Wrong beliefs can have varied sources of authority. Wrong beliefs will allow you permission to do whatever is trendy, whatever is popular, whatever is fashionable, and whatever is the latest.

The DL is one of a myriad of things that is categorized under wrong authority. Why is it that men are sleeping with men? More than that, how can a man live as an espionage agent by having sexual and intimate affections for a man and a woman? Why is it that this DL thing is catching on like wild fire? *What's up with the Down Low?*

Years ago, for the most part, anyone who was thought of as homosexual was scorned by society. It did not make a difference whether or not you were black or white, rich or poor, fat or skinny; it was an indictment to be labeled homosexual. Anyone who was considered queer was shunned by society. In fact, it was not that long ago that we heard about people who were coming out of the proverbial closet. As I thought about the "come out of the closet" movement, I asked myself a few rhetorical questions. Why are people coming out of the closet? Why were they in the closet in the first place? What were they doing in the closet? Well, it is simple. They were in the closet because they were afraid of being labeled. Labeled what? They were afraid of being labeled abominable.

Homosexuality was considered abominable socially and more so biblically. Who wants to be classified as being abominable? The fact that many were in the closet typifies that something was wrong in the first place. The reason why so many have come out of the closet is that society has made a grand attempt to alleviate the stigma of homosexuality being abominable both secularly and biblically. Unfortunately, it appears that society's attempt is working.

Many DL brothers are married, have children, attend church, are respected among their peers and community, and are highly successful. If this describes you, I am sad to say, you are living a brick-veneered life. If you have ever seen a brick-veneered house, it is a house with brick in the front but not in the back. A brick-veneered house is a house that gives the impression from a frontal perspective that the entire house is uniform (brick). However, when you take a glance at the house from another perspective you will discover that the sides and the back do not match the front. Any man who can be married to a woman, have children, and sleep with other men is a veneered person. If you are living this veneered lifestyle without seeing anything wrong with it, you are a person who is operating under the wrong authority. You are a person who makes your own rules, draws your own boundaries, and have become your own referee.

In the book of Genesis, it was not long after man was created that he became contaminated with sin. When God breathed into the nostrils of man, he came alive both physically and spiritually. Once man was alive, he became God-conscious. The fact that the Scriptures inform us that man was created in the image and likeness of God meant that man had the moral capability and aptitude to understand what God expected out of his life.

Unfortunately, no sooner was man created than he willfully fell from grace. Why did he fall? He fell because he disobeyed the mandate of a holy God by eating the forbidden fruit. When man and woman took of the forbidden fruit, all hell broke loose. From that day to this, every time mankind leaps across the fence into restricted areas things get worse. The simple sin of partaking of the forbidden fruit busted Pandora's Box wide open to every sin imaginable. There was a time when people were shocked, stunned, and surprised about the things that came from Pandora's Box, but those days are swiftly passing away. Things that once amazed us no longer amaze us. Why is that? We are anesthetized to all the things that were once taboo. This has caused us to lose dominion. The reason there are fewer taboos in this generation as opposed to the last one is that each generation gets a little more lax in their moral aptitude and aspirations.

In Ecclesiastes 7:29, King Solomon, the son of David, makes a profound statement about dominion that has gone bad. The verse reads: *Truly, this only have I found: That God made man upright, But they have sought out many schemes.*

The book of Ecclesiastes is a book by which Solomon attempted, through a series of searches, to find out things that would bring him satisfaction. He experimented with everything under the sun to see if any of it would bring him satisfaction and enjoyment.

He tried science, the study of the natural law of the universe. He studied philosophy and psychology only to find out that it is one thing to be challenged psychologically and socially, but it is another thing to be challenged spiritually. Solomon tried the gamut of materialism and pleasure—still no satisfaction. Wine, women, wealth, religion, fatalism were just a few things that were tested in his labyrinth of living. However, complete satisfaction was absent from all. In the final stage of his search, Solomon began to look at morality.

Ecclesiastes 7:29 declares, ...*God made man upright, but they have sought out many schemes.* Notice, man had evolved into something that God did not create. In Luke 19, after Jesus made his coronation ride into the city of Jerusalem, he walked into the temple. Once in the temple He overturned tables and threw the moneychangers out of the temple because of their defiling practices. As Jesus ran the moneychangers out of the temple, He stated in verse 46, *It is written, my house is a house of prayer, but you have made it a den of thieves.*

Whatever your home is today, it has become that because that is what you have made it. Whatever your marriage has become today, it has become that because of what you have made it. Whatever your church is today, it has become that because that is what you have made it. Whatever secret DL lifestyle you have, you have it because that is what you have made. If you live a DL lifestyle but do not see yourself as being gay, you have created that lifestyle. For DL men to pride themselves on always having a woman in their life, in spite of sleeping with men, is a sinful promiscuous pride to have.

Being a good person, a law-abiding citizen, a community activist and a myriad of other things are simply not enough. All of the aforementioned things usually serve as a pseudo pacifier that enables a DL man to continue to live behind a straw wall of self.

Whatever man has become, he has become that because he has changed what God made. Three things will cause you to stray from dominion:

1. The first thing that will cause you to stray from dominion is *Spiritual Perversion.*

Spiritual perversion occurs when a man becomes amoral and amiss. *Amoral* means that you are "neither moral nor immoral. It means that you are outside the sphere to which moral judgment applies."[3] When a man reaches this state, he becomes anesthetized or numb to the things that are wrong. The word *amiss* means "to go astray."[4] People consumed with spiritual perversion are people that have not only lost dominion, but they are people who have a manufactured zeal about both God and morality. This manufactured zeal usually results in a void spiritual knowledge. Whenever a man comes up with his own ideology of who God is outside of the perimeters of God's Word, he creates his own form of godliness.

In the tenth chapter of the book of Romans, the apostle Paul addressed his Jewish counterparts who were misguided. Romans 10:1-3 reads: *Brethren, my heart's desire and prayer to God for Israel is that they may be saved. For I bear them witness that they have a zeal for God, but not according to knowledge. For they being ignorant of God's righteousness, and seeking to establish their own righteousness, have not submitted to the righteousness of God.*

Having a zeal of God without knowledge causes one to come up with his own ideology of what life is and what life is not. Since we live in a self-righteous society, it becomes easier to march to the beat of a different drum. In some areas of this country, it has become acceptable for two men or two women to raise a child. At the rate we are going, soon it will be okay for adults to sleep with children as long as both parties consent.

Now, we have DL men who feel they are neither gay nor wrong because they like a little "spice" on the side. What in the world is going on? Man has lost the dominion given to him by God.

Paul states in Romans 10:3 that people who are ignorant of God's righteousness sought to create their own form of righteousness so they do not have to submit to the righteousness of God. Whenever you come up with your personal ideology of God outside of the parameter of the Word of God, you create your own form of righteousness.

Too many people are confusing the love of God with the justice of God. According to Romans 5:8, *But God showed his great love for us by sending Christ to die for us while we were still sinners,* the love of God is unconditional. Regardless of what you have done in the past, God loves you just as you are. If you are an alcoholic, lesbian, homosexual, pedophile, or pervert, God loves you. This verse states that while we were "still sinners" Christ died for us. However, we must never confuse God's love with God's justice.

I have four wonderful children. I love them so much that I will discipline them when they are wrong. God is the same way. It is because of His love for us that He extends His rod of correction to us. Parents who do not establish boundaries, parameters, and guidelines for their children are setting them up for failure. Keep in mind that energy with no direction leads to chaos. Whenever there is the absence of parental guidance in a child's life, failure is inevitable. No parent, in their right mind, observing a child stealing Snickers® out of the grocery store, would allow this crime to go unpunished. No decent parents would willfully sit by idly while their eight-year-old pocketed another kid's property without addressing the matter. Any parent who does not reprimand, rebuke, correct, or chastise a child who has done wrong is aiding and abetting them in trespassing the law.

If God sat by silently and did nothing while humanity does its thing, God would be aiding and abetting our sins. That's not God. He loves us so much that when we are wrong, He chastises us so that we may live right. In order for you to have an adequate theory of God, you must understand the premise of His Word. There is a slogan that says, "If it feels good do it." Unfortunately, the feeling, which has been so good, is now spreading AIDS. The feeling now has many people infected.

2. The next thing that has caused man to lose dominion is *Sexual Perversion.*

Sexual Perversion involves sexual preferences and sexual prefabrication. Many of the sexual odysseys that have confronted society today have come from an unbridled imagination. Why is it that no one has ever seen a man in the maternity ward who has given birth to a baby? This has never happened because God did not give men the plumbing that would bring forth babies; He gave them the plumbing that would produce life.

One of the purposes for which men and women were created was procreation. In order for procreation to occur, you need a man and a woman. This is the original plan of God. When you substitute the original ordained plan of God with an alternate plan, the substitute will neither compare nor compete with the original.

Sexual Preferences are sexual desires, fantasies, dreams and escapades that one prefers. The reason man has lost dominion is because he no longer lives his life or raises his children according to the statutes and the principles of Judeo Christian beliefs. The reason God ordained Adam and Eve and not Adam and Steve is because He intended for balance to be in the home. On one hand, there is sugar, spice, and everything nice and on the other hand there must be a voice of authority.

Since everyone has come up with his own thing, we now have two women raising children, and two men raising children.

Sexual Prefabrications are sexual fantasies invented and created in the mind. In Romans 1:26, we get a vivid biblical understanding of what God thinks about people who are consumed by Sexual Perversion. The Scripture reads, *For this reason God gave them up to vile passions. For even their women exchanged the natural use for what is against nature.* This verse refers to unnatural sexual relations between persons of the same sex.

Lesbianism, homosexuality, and DL relationships are all against nature because these relationships are contrary to the will of God's divine intent. Even the lowest form of creatures that God created seek after the opposite sex.

According to the Word of God, it is unnatural for a man to desire to be rubbed up by another man. Verse 27 reads, *Likewise also the men, leaving the natural use of the woman, burned in their lust for one another, men with men committing what is shameful, and receiving in themselves the penalty of their error which was due.*

This verse serves as the icing on the cake pertaining to why man has lost dominion. This verse personifies a person who has put the script of God's Word down while picking up his own script. Verse 27 conveys the fact that there were men consumed with total perversion of their natural function. As they turned away from what God ordained (man and woman), they burned for the desire to be with a man. Any man who has a woman in his life, or no woman in his life, and desires to be with a man is a man who is burning with lust.

The spirit of perversion is never satisfied with getting its client to the first stage of perversion. The spirit of perversion desires to take its client as far and as long as one would like to travel. The spirit of perversion is a spirit of lust. If lust is not quickly held in check, it will cause you to lose all sense of reason and rationale.

The problem with many DL men is that they think with the wrong head. In the heat of the moment, emotion will shut down your thinking head. When lust is not placed in check, the smaller head will begin to speak louder than the larger head, causing you to follow a feeling rather than facts. As long as you are fighting the feeling, you are all right. If you are fighting the feeling to be with someone of the same sex, this is a good thing. When you refuse to act on those feelings, it means that God is aiding you in keeping your emotions in check.

It is the devil's major aim to get you to the point that you no longer fight against that which you know is wrong. The reason many DL brothers do not let people know that they are on the DL is because they know it is wrong. A DL lifestyle is a life that is filled with lies, acting, mannequins and masquerades. Once you have given into the lifestyle, you will still feel awkward because it was never designed by God to be natural.

3. The last thing that is responsible for man losing his dominion is *Psychological Perversion.*

Solomon said in Ecclesiastes 7:29, *that man was made upright, nevertheless he sought out many schemes or inventions.* Man was so disgruntled with what God created for him that he came up with his own standard and boundaries for life. Psychological Perversion deals with perverted thinking and perverted theology. Do you know why God destroyed the world the first time? Genesis 6:5, 6 reads, *Then the LORD saw that the wickedness of man was great in the earth, and that every intent of the thoughts of his heart was only evil continually. And the LORD was sorry that He had made man on the earth, and He was grieved in His heart.*

These verses reveal that God was overwhelmingly disappointed in man's behavior. Man's destruction came as a result of his traveling further and further away from a holy God. Whenever man is left to himself, he will eventually destroy himself.

Some of what we are getting is a result of many parents who are not schooling their children about the game of life. Many parents today are trying, so desperately, to be friends with their children as opposed to being parents. Parents who allow their children to have sleep-in boyfriends and girlfriends are feeding a beast whose appetite will only increase. The reason society treats women as if they are "hoochies" is because we allow our girls to leave the house looking like hoochies.

I have discovered in life that people will treat you in the same manner you treat yourself. Your apparel says a lot about you. There was a time when a man would have to imagine what a girl had. That day is over; many girls today are guilty of revealing all of Georgia and Mississippi.

Nowadays, it is virtually impossible to watch a rap video on BET or VH1 without seeing black folks in demeaning positions. It only takes watching a few of these videos to recognize that there is a common thread that runs throughout all of them. That common thread is the harem. Almost every flick has the bling-bling, plush cribs, pimped out rides, and booty-shaking gyrating women.

The message, subliminal and overt, is both detrimental and destructive to everything that is wholesome. The sexual overtures and open promiscuity are pulverizing every moral and decent fiber of our country.

Just about every rapper will have at least fifteen to twenty girls in his video gyrating, moving, dancing, sitting in a hot tub and the list goes on. The reason all of the girls are in the video is because "you ain't mackin if your flick ain't stackin." Any girl who watches this trash daily might soon find it acceptable to be a part of a harem. As for the boys who view this foolishness, these videos serve as nothing more than a "wild oats" sowing license.

The fact that the Scripture declares that man was made upright simply means he was made with truth, equity, and morals. Nevertheless, man has toiled to create another lifestyle. Instead of man following God's prescribed course, man has chosen to go in his own direction.

Romans 1:28 reads, *And even as they did not like to retain God in their knowledge, God gave them over to a debased mind, to do those things which are not fitting…* This verse reveals that the mind that cannot, or will not, perceive God, will equate to spiritual death. Why is it that there are people who choose not to retain God in their knowledge?

The word *debase* in verse 28 is another word for *reprobate*. The word *reprobate* comes from the Greek word *adokimos*, which means "unapproved, unworthy, and unacceptable toward God." The word *mind* comes from the Greek word *nous*, which consists of your mental perception or the central of your intelligence[5] What this passage is saying is that a mind that will so disrespectfully and blatantly reject God, will be permitted to do what it wants without moral consciousness.

When you want to do what you want to do, you do not want anything to remind you that what you are doing is wrong. God is a God of compassion. For those of you who are struggling with a DL lifestyle, homosexuality, lesbianism, or promiscuity, God loves you just as you are. If you feel nasty, filthy, dirty, or unclean when you act upon these unnatural feelings, this is a great indication that you still possess some form of God-consciousness. It is also a good indication that God has not given up on you. Keep fighting the feeling. Know that what you are doing is wrong. Turn that problem over to God, and get your mind renewed every day.

Lord, bless those who struggle with unnatural feelings.

Everybody's Doing It

That's a Lie!

People often excuse or justify immoral behavior with the attitude that "everybody's doing it." The society we reside in willfully admits that it does what it does because "everybody's doing it." Why is it that morals, values, and virtues play a diminishing role in our society? Unfortunately, social acceptance has become the order of the day.

Not long ago I was having a father-and-son debate with one of my sons. As we talked with each other, our conversation led to an impasse of opinions. The focus of our stalemate was a toy that we saw on TV. While waiting for the sitcom we were watching to return, a commercial aired that showed a boy playing with a toy. Within a fraction of a second after the commercial went off, my son asked me if I would buy him that toy. Waiting for a response, I cautiously, methodically, and diligently explained to him all the reasons why I did not think that he should have that type of toy. I went on to convey other reasons why I thought purchasing this particular toy was a bad idea.

I thought I had presented my case well but before I could finish, he responded by saying, "The little boy on TV has one." That was the whole argument. It didn't matter what I said, how adequately I explained values, or what type of fatherly advice I gave him, all he knew was he was justified and vindicated in his desires because somebody "else was doing it."

One must be ever mindful to guard his or her mind from the pollutants of life. Perhaps you did not know, but just as an idle mind is a playground for the devil, a weak mind provides the picnic on the playground. Bad habits have a way of controlling a weak mind. It is for that reason that you must fight the good fight of faith.

In order to play any game competitively one must first learn the rules. Any person desiring to receive the prize at the end of the day must do it lawfully by adhering to the regulation and governance of that particular game. All lawful games have two things in common: a rules book and a referee. If all the participants in life would govern themselves, be truthful in all that they did, and be honest about the infraction they made, there would be no need for governance.

Why are there so many laws, rules, and regulations? Where did all these "thou shalt" and "thou shalt not" come from? Believe it or not, many of them came from the Word of God. My friend, whether you know it or not, God is a God of order. God is the one who established government. In the heavenly realm, the Bible speaks of angels, archangels, seraphim, and cherubs. In the demonic realm, there are principalities, powers, rulers of darkness, and spiritual wickedness in high places. In the earthly realm, God chose man to be both head and priest of his family.

With headship, God bequeathed authority. With great authority comes great responsibility and with great responsibility comes great authority. As God made and established man as the priest of the home, man was not given a position for the purpose of him doing what he wanted to do; rather it was for the purpose of doing what God wanted him to do. Any time a man is unfaithful to his spouse, whether he is a DL brother or a gigolo, he has abused his God-given authority.

It was God and not man who set up the institution of marriage. It was God who said that a man shall leave father and mother, cleave to his wife, and they shall become one flesh.

To leave and to cleave means to be a one-woman man. I wonder how many women would have married a DL brother had they known about his clandestine life style either prior to their marriage or the day of the marriage? I wonder what woman in her right mind would knowingly marry a man who is seeking out other men to sleep with on the side. I wonder what woman in her right mind would tell her husband on their wedding night that as long as you are a good provider, a good father, a member in good standing with the church, and an outstanding citizen of the community, I don't mind you living a DL lifestyle. Isn't that absurd! The reason brothers are on the DL is because they know it is not right. As you read this book, know that it is my intent to be convictive and not condescending. A DL lifestyle is a masquerade. It is a sham! It is a marriage on paper but not in practice; it is based on lies and not loyalty, and it is self-serving and not family sensitive.

DL bothers are brothers who march to a different beat. DL brothers are brothers that play with a different rulebook. Many DL brothers don't consider themselves gay because they have a wife, children, are members in good standing with their church, and are respected in their community. Each one of these components is a small piece of facade that has been established to cleanse the conscience for having illicit feelings and committing illicit acts.

Now that the DL brothers' network has grown and is more exposed, many are feeling a little more at ease about their sexuality, knowing that many more people feel the way they feel and are doing what they are doing. Now that we all know someone who is either gay or DL, this makes it easier for the man who is struggling with his DL lifestyle to be DL because "everybody is doing it." Although we say, "everybody is doing it" that is but a false notion. Everybody is not doing it! Usually, when we say that everybody is doing it, we are looking through the magnifying glass of the devil. An imprint in small writing on the passenger side of my truck says, "Objects may seem closer than they appear." The mirror reads this because the manufacturer of the truck placed a magnifying mirror there.

Satan is the manufacturer of sin. He is the father of all lies, a slanderer, and an accuser of the brethren. Although it appears that "everybody's doing it," remember everybody's not doing it. If you think that everybody is doing it, it may be because you are seeing life through the devil's mirror.

Perhaps you are wondering why I have referenced God and Scripture in this book. If you have noticed this, this is by design.

Did you know that the sex drive is one of the strongest drives or desires known to man? Why do you think that prostitution is one of the oldest professions around? Why is pornography a multibillion dollar industry? Why these phenomena? People are sexually out of control.

Constantly and consistently, every day, we are faced with sexual overtures. Commercials involving sodas, cars, chewing gum, tennis shoes, clothes, and videos are sprinkled with accents of sex. Why such a barrage of sex? Well, everybody knows that sex sells. Sex sells because it is one of mankind's strongest desires. Since sex brands a strong desire, in order to conquer the desire it is imperative that you possess something that is stronger than what possesses you. Your solution is the Word of God, not a prayer cloth, a bunch of Jesus jargon, catchy church phrases, seed offerings, or anything else. In plain and simple terms, it is the unadulterated Word of God.

I believe there are many DL bothers who attend church. Many of these men attend church for different reasons. Some attend because they are on the hunt; others are looking for deliverance, while the remaining brothers attend so that they may appease their consciences and maintain a form of godliness. It is imperative that you recognize that being a regular church attendee, a church member, or even an officer in a local church does not equate to God sanctioning your behavior. Many DL brothers, whether they admit it or not, are looking for sanctioning from as many possible venues as possible, especially from the church.

The homosexual, lesbian, and DL brother who attends church on a regular basis are generally attracted to churches with an affinity for their lifestyle. Unfortunately, there are many churches in America that are loving people right into hell because they are revealing to their congregants a one-sided Jesus. Many churches have the idea that in order to get along you must go along. Beyond any doubt, the Scripture reveals that God is both a God of love and judgment. If you present people the loving aspect of God without the justice aspect of God, in essence, you are not presenting God at all. When alternative life styles are "sanctioned" by the church or a denomination, this gives a greater credence for DL behavior, homosexuality and lesbianism. The Episcopalian church is at odds with the ordination of a gay man who has been appointed bishop in the Episcopalian church. Bishop V. Gene Robinson has shared that he has been with the man in his life for at least thirteen years. By his point of view, he is in a monogamous relationship.[6]

What have we come to? What are we doing? It appears that the more outlandish things are, the more they become acceptable in the eyes of society. America has attempted to get a drink of water from a fire hydrant, and she has gotten her head blown off. It is impossible to live life without morals, values, governance, boundaries and parameters without being classified as a renegade.

An amazing thing occurred in the 35th chapter of the book of Jeremiah. Judah (the chosen people of God), through rebellion and disobedience, had become estranged from God. Therefore, God sent Jeremiah to teach them a valuable lesson about loyalty. God had Jeremiah go to the package store, purchase some wine and invite the Rechabites (Jeremiah 35:2) to come over and have a drink. When the Rechabites were offered wine for their consumption, they refused the offer; of course, this was of no surprise to God. What was it that caused the Rechabites to reject Jeremiah's offer? It was a covenant established by their ancestors that no Rechabite was to partake of strong drink. Although years had passed since the covenant was established, the Rechabites held true to form to the family customs and traditions of their ancestors. God was driving the point home to Judah that if a family can remain loyal to their heritage, then people who supposedly love and serve God ought to be able to do even more.

Perhaps as you are reading this book you are thinking that the feelings you have for another man are so strong that you have no other choice but to submit to those feelings. Maybe your craving to be with a man has grown to the point that your sexual appetite is insatiable. On the other hand, maybe you are at that point and place in your life that you have concluded that this is the way God made you; therefore, whoever accepts it or rejects it, that is their problem.

I do not know whether someone has told you, but you can live a life that is pleasing to God, joyful to you, and complete in nature if you do three things:

1. Walk in the Word of God
2. Walk in the Wisdom of God
3. Walk in the Will of God

The reason the nation of Judah suffered from the "can't help its" is because they didn't walk according to the Word of God. The city of Jerusalem and the nation of Judah became saturated with sin because the Word of God was not held at the forefront of the people's hearts and minds. The impending and proverbial wheel of justice was set in motion. If Judah would repent, God would both forgive and bless them; however, a lack of repentance brought forth judgment. God purposely and deliberately allowed Judah to go into captivity because they refused to follow the prescribed mandate of His Word. Their rebellion netted them bondage.

Although they possessed the Spirit of God and had the Word of God as a compass, they chose to chart their own course and navigate through the issues of life by their own prescriptions. Judah's first failure, as a nation, stemmed from not walking in the Word of God, and their next failure stemmed from not walking in the wisdom of God. Keep in mind that wisdom is knowledge applied. The story of Judah is a classic case that illustrates that just because you know better does not mean that you will do better.

Judah's abandonment of the things of God parallels that of our society today. Judah listened to the wrong voices and pursued the wrong people to mirror how they live their lives. They were well aware of what God expected of them; nevertheless, they chose to live a perverted lifestyle.

The Bible is very clear and fixed on its position about promiscuity, adultery, fornication, and homosexuality. The nation of Judah was well aware of the Word of God and the heart of God; however, they chose to go in a different direction. Having an awareness of the Word of God and following the Word of God are two different things.

Having the ability to quote Psalm 23 *(The Lord is my shepherd…)* will not make the Lord your shepherd. It takes more than knowing where John 3:16 is in the Bible to save you from hell, fire and brimstone. The only thing that will make the Lord your shepherd, keep you from hell, fire and brimstone, is the application of the Word of God.

Anytime a person can practice a sinful lifestyle and sit in church on a regular basis, without any moral convictions, it is a result of one or two things. Either the preaching has become cold or you have become calloused. Possessing the knowledge of God's Word without the application of God's Word equates to defeat.

The final thing that rendered Judah helpless, as far as walking in the Word of God, was that they got in the way of God. As a DL brother, you will never be able to walk in the ways of God until you get out of the way of God. When you are in the way, God cannot perform the things He would desire to do in your life.

As a kid growing up, one of the joys in life was walking up to the confectionary store to buy candy. In the store, there were many different assortments of candy. One of my favorites was Lemon Heads®. The hard yellow candy was sour on the outside and sweet on the inside. As a kid, I practically never took the time to analyze candy because I was too busy eating it. Now that I have grown up, I analyze things a lot more. As a kid, I used to think that a Lemon Head® was one piece of hard candy, but now I know that it is actually two pieces of candy.

An outer layer of sour candy is placed over an inner core of sweet candy. The candy was actually two pieces that appeared to be one piece. Lemon Heads® typify the DL lifestyle. The only difference is that the outer layer represents the sweetness while the inner core represents the sour.

As a kid, both my friends and I knew what we were getting when we bought Lemon Heads®. We were well aware that once we opened that box and popped a few of those bad boys in our mouths, we would squirm for a while and make all types of funny faces until we got through the sour part. Once we made it through the sour part, we would enjoy the sweet part.

Unfortunately, when a woman hooks up with a DL brother she doesn't *know what she is getting into. What is often so devastating to women who fall in love with* DL brothers is that they do not know that they've bargained for a box of Lemon Heads®. Unfortunately, everything that appears to be sweet about their spouse is actually a sweet facade placarded around a sour life. To DL brothers, a wife, a child, church affiliation, and community respect are nothing more than pawns in the picture of sour secrets.

A vow is an oath. When you marry a woman, you give an oath that you will love her, honor her, keep her in sickness and in health until death do you part. When married men embark upon excursions looking for men to sleep with, something is drastically wrong.

The nation of Judah failed because they got in the way of God. Whenever you do what you desire as opposed to what God has prescribed, you will always find yourself not being able to experience God's blessings because you are in the way.

When Love Is Wrong

*Do not love the world or the things in the world. If any-
one loves the world, the love of the Father is not in him.
For all that is in the world—the lust of the flesh, the
lust of the eyes, and the pride of life—is not of the
Father but is of the world. And the world is passing
away, and the lust of it; but he who does the will of God
abides forever (1 John 2:15-20).*

Luther Ingram, one of the great songsters of the 70s, bel-
lowed out a song about infidelity that rose to the top of
the music charts in that era. The name of the song was, "If
Loving You Is Wrong, I Don't Want to be Right." This chart-
buster hit the billboards like a sledgehammer. The song was
centered around a married man that had become intimate
with another woman. The man had grown so attached to his

mistress that despite his parents' verbal disapproval of his affair, the desire to be with his mistress outweighed the respect and sentiments of his parents. The man had become so enamored that he was willing to go to great lengths in order to keep the fling intact. Some of the friends of the mistress said that a relationship between a married man and a single woman was futile. However, despite all of the pressure to do the right thing, the man stated that he did not want to be right. A lifestyle based solely on feeling and not on moral fundamentals typifies a train wreck waiting to happen.

The "if it feels good, do it mentality" is an attitude that defies everything that is wholesome and morally right. Whether you are a DL brother or just your typical player, the path you blaze today will become the path that the next generation will follow tomorrow.

If being promiscuous or living a DL life style is so hip, cool, or en vogue, why don't we teach it to our children? Why don't we teach our little girls that it's okay to be loved by a man who sleeps with men, just as long as he provides for you, takes the garbage out, buys you seafood dinners, attends church with you, and makes love to you occasionally? Since the DL lifestyle is such the happening thing, why don't we start teaching our boys, at an early age, how to be clever and cunning, camouflagers of truth? Why not teach them at a young age how to hold down a man and a woman at the same time?

My friend, anyone that will go to great lengths to lie about one area of his or her life will go to great lengths to lie about any other area of their life. For those DL brothers who are dating or married to women, to all the people in your circle of influence, your life is nothing more than a game of charades. The travesty of your entire life is centered on how the men you screw around with know more of your dark secrets than the people you supposedly love the most.

To be frank with you, the DL lifestyle in all actuality is a "low down" lifestyle. It is mighty "low down" to make a woman think that she is your only squeeze, only to find out that you have been squeezing some dude. The other thing that makes the DL the *LD* is the fact that some of the men you are having encounters with are men from different walks and venues of life. Some are having sexual encounters with men they either half know, or just met. For those who have known their male counterparts for a period of time, your actions are not excused either.

Any girl or woman who will sleep with a man she barely knows, or has just met, is quickly labeled a whore. Any man who has a smidgen of decency in him would never marry a girl when he knows that all the guys in his neighborhood have slept with her. Can you imagine a guy attempting to introduce his fiancée to all of his buddies, and they tell him, "We already know who she is because we all have slept with her."

As a DL brother, can you imagine someone approaching your wife saying, "You and John make a wonderful couple, and by the way, thank you for allowing John and me to spend time together doing the wild thing." Friend, it is my earnest prayer that you will not only examine your life but also come to grips with the error of your ways. It is my sincere prayer that this book will challenge you to begin to take a good look at your life. In the Gospel of John chapter 10 and verse 10, Jesus stated, *The thief does not come except to steal, and to kill, and to destroy. I have come that they may have life, and that they may have it more abundantly.* What John is actually saying is that the devil comes to bring destruction. Whether through lies, deception, or betrayal, his one aim in life is to destroy families, relationships, bonds, covenants, and integrity. On the contrary, Jesus desires that we may have the abundant life. The abundant life means that through Christ you can experience the joy and bliss of having both fellowship and relationship with Him in time and through eternity.

As some of you read this book, I recognize that you are struggling with everything within you to battle against the feeling and the desire of being with another man. In your heart of hearts, you know that the feelings and inclinations you have toward the same sex is inordinate. I commend you in Christ and pray that God will give you the tools and strength to overcome those tendencies as you continue to read this book and most of all trust God and read His Word.

While some of you are struggling with your feelings, others of you have already surrendered to your feelings. As far as you are concerned, this book is nothing more than another book that bashes gay or lesbian people. Either you will shelve or, more than likely, trash this book because you consider me an antiquated relic who is not apprised of the changing trends of society.

This chapter is dedicated to those of you who are struggling to do what is right and who are seeking the face of God. In order to get help as you struggle with your feelings, you must first and foremost, get rid of all of your crutches. As you gravitate toward true manhood, you must leave behind every crutch you have used through the years to justify your affinity for men. "God made me this way." "Why did God make me this way?" "I've been feeling like this for years." 'I was molested as a child." "Someone turned me on to porn as a child." "If God did not want me to be gay, He would have made me straight." All of these crutches and a myriad of others will grant you permission to live a gay, lesbian or DL lifestyle.

Maybe you have never heard this, but God never created a homosexual, a lesbian, a DL brother, a whore, gang banger, pimp, pusher, or serial killer. The Word of God does inform us of what God did create. He created a man and a woman. When

God created Adam (man) and Eve (woman), they were innocent in God's sight as well as in their own sight. What was it
that changed their state of innocence? What changed their
innocence was that Adam and Eve did what they felt like doing
as opposed to what God said.

In the second chapter of Genesis, God explicitly told Adam
that he and Eve had the freedom to eat freely of any tree in
Eden with the exception of the Tree of Knowledge of Good
and Evil. God gave a cosmic caveat when He told Adam, "The
day you eat of this tree, you will surely die." When God made
Adam, He made him a free moral agent. This meant that
Adam was not a robot and he had the ability to choose to do
what God said or not. If he chose to do what God said, he
would experience the joy of God, if not, he would experience
the judgment of God. When Adam chose not to obey, the rest
is history. God kicked both Adam and Eve out of paradise.

Every time we disobey God's Word, we suffer the consequences of God's judgment. After Adam and Eve were kicked
out of Eden, they had two sons: Cain and Abel. Cain was a
farmer and Abel a shepherd. The book of Genesis reveals that
at certain times both boys would offer sacrifices to the Lord.
The biblical account of Genesis also reveals that although God
was pleased with Abel's offering, He was displeased with Cain's
offering. Therefore, God rejected Cain's offering. As a result of
having his sacrifice rejected, Cain got mad (jealous) with his
brother because God favored his sacrifice. Cain got so mad he
killed Abel.

What was it that caused Cain to kill his brother? Did Cain
kill his brother because God made him a murderer? Was Cain
born a murderer? Had he been exposed to drive-by shootings
as a kid? Keep in mind there were no movies or videos to influence him. There were no programs such as CSI, America's
Most Wanted, or COPS. In the early days of creation, there

were no gang bangers, thugs, pedophilia, or prostitution. What was it that caused Cain to murder his brother? The answer is summed up in one word, "sin"! Sin grants you permission to operate on feelings as opposed to moral fundamentals. Cain killed his brother because he felt like doing it. My friend, the reason you feel the way you feel and do what you do is not because God made you that way, it is because of your "sin nature."

When Adam and Eve opened up Pandora's Box, all hell broke loose. As a matter of fact, things got so bad that God destroyed the world by a flood because He said that man's thoughts were continually evil (Genesis 6). How did people in the early days of creation know how to do so much evil? Once the mother and father of all living ate of the forbidden fruit, man's evil imagination ran the gamut. The "feel good mentality" or the "just do it" philosophy didn't start with Nike, it started in the early days of creation.

My friend, if you want to know why your feelings are being toyed with like a puppet on a string, it's because Satan is appealing to your flesh. As human beings, we all suffer from different physical inclinations. Some adults have the inclination to sleep with children. Others have a fetish for men. Then there are those who are married but choose to tip out on their wives. Think about it, if everyone acted on their feelings or did what they felt like doing, the world would be in anarchy. Every day there are people who undress other people and have sex with them in their mind. What if those thoughts were actually carried out? Rape and molestation in America would be unprecedented. My friend, doing what you feel is not an excuse to act upon those feelings. My words of encouragement to you are, "**Keep fighting the feeling.**"

Many of you who are reading this book are saved, but unfortunately, you are influenced by Luther Ingram's song,

("If Loving You Is Wrong, I Don't Want to be Right"). Despite knowing what is right, you move solely on your feelings, even wrong feelings. Knowing better does not necessarily equate to doing better.

In the first epistle (letter) of John, John tells the reader how those who accept Christ can really know that they are children of God. John states that you can know that you are a child of God by loving Him and by keeping His commandments. As John speaks about the commandments, he is not talking about the Ten Commandments; rather he is speaking of all the commandments that Jesus gave.

1 John 2:15 states, *Do not love the world or the things in the world. If anyone loves the world, the love of the Father is not in him.* As John makes a reference to the world, he is not talking about physical creation. Nor is he speaking of the world of humanity or mankind. The Greek word for "world" here is *kosmos.*[7] Although the word does not always have a negative connotation, here it means world system, the organized system headed by Satan, which leaves God out and is actually opposed to Him.

In John 14:30 Jesus said, *I will no longer talk much with you, for the ruler of this world is coming, and he has nothing in Me.* Jesus was actually saying that the prince of this world wanted nothing to do with him. To act worldly means that you act as though God is not your Father. Ephesians 2:2 declares, *In which you once walked according to the course of this world, according to the prince of the power of the air, the spirit who now works in the sons of disobedience.*

What is the course of this world? Greed, selfish ambition, deceit, orgies, homosexuality, lesbianism, adultery, gossip, sedition, and the DL lifestyle are all part of the course of this world. Galatians 6:14 reads, *But God forbid that I should boast except in the cross of our Lord Jesus Christ, by whom the world has been crucified to me, and I to the world."* What is the point Paul is attempting to drive home? He is simply saying that standing between him and a satanic world is a cross. Although both are bidding, he can only have one Lord.

In order for your practice to line up with your position in Christ, you need the cleansing power of the Holy Spirit to wash the world out of your life so that you will not become wishy-washy in your walk. This can only occur when you separate from the world and the things of the world.

In the latter part of verse 15 of 1 John 2, John addresses those who really love the world. The expression "If any man loves the world" is a hypothetical condition in the subjunctive mode. The verb is in the present tense. John could have used the aorist tense, expressing merely the fact of loving the world.[8] However, he goes out of the way to use the present tense, which tense in the subjunctive modes (expresses the mood) always stresses continuation, habitual action. Since the world is evil, believers that follow the system of the world rebel against the Word of God.

Whenever there is rebellion against the things of God, there will always be a reproach. God is offended when we rebel because He knows that through our rebellion we dig ourselves in a hole that we cannot get out of. What happens when a father warns his son not to do drugs, but he does it anyway? The kid must fight addiction for the rest of his life.

What happens to the young girl whose mother told her not to become sexually active, but the girl negates the info, gets pregnant, and takes on a responsibility that she will have for the rest of her life? Instead of enjoying her teenage years, she has to focus on being a mother and raising a child. Many times, we go astray from the will of God because we don't have anything in us that keeps us restrained.

In verse 16, John addresses a trinity of depravity. The lust of the flesh, the lust of the eyes, and the pride of life serve as a hodgepodge of natural evil manifestation. The lust of the flesh is the passionate desire and impulses we receive from our nature—all those things that excite and inflame the pleasures of the flesh.

The world is obliged whenever you surrender to its vices. If you came to Jesus with a vice, He can, will, and is able to give you the power to overcome it. As Christ extends an invitation for you to come to Him like you are, you need to know that His invitation was not extended so you could remain as you are. The only way to overcome the vices of your life is to have your mind renewed every single day (Roman 12:1,2).

Since the eyes are the windows of the flesh, when your mind is unrenewed, your eyes will always be drawn to your flesh and fleshly addictions. Remember the world is obliged when you give in to the lust of the flesh, the lust of the eyes, and the pride of life. The pride of life represents your status in the world. It represents positions, plateaus, and places.

Physics has a theory called the Second Law of Thermodynamics. The Second Law of Thermodynamics describes basic principles familiar in everyday life. It is partially a universal law of decay, the ultimate cause of why everything ultimately falls apart and disintegrates over time. Material things are not eternal. Everything appears to change eventually and chaos increases. Nothing stays as fresh as the day one buys it; clothing becomes faded, threadbare, and ultimately returns to dust. Everything ages and wears out. Even death is a manifestation of this law. The effects of the Second Law are all around, touching everything in the universe.[9]

When a bank is on the brink of becoming insolvent, wise people do not deposit money in it. When a home is built with faulty material, it is a matter of time before the home collapses. When we live according to our dictates, wishes, and whims, in a spiritual sense, we engage the Second Law of Thermodynamics in our lives. Focusing on this world is like fighting for a first class seat on the *Titanic*.

chapter
FOUR

Exchanging the Truth

Not long ago the Harvey Milk High School, an expansion of a 1984 city program consisting of two small classrooms for gay students, would enroll about a hundred students and would open in the fall. ABC news reported that the mayor of New York, Michael Bloomberg, along with the administration thought that this was a good idea. The school is named after San Francisco's first openly gay city supervisor, Harvey Milk, who was assassinated in 1978 along with George Mascone.[10]

On Monday, August 4, 2003, the House of Deputies of the Anglican Church (Episcopal), a legislative body composed of clergy and lay people, voted to approve the Rev. V. Gene Robinson (a gay man) as bishop of New Hampshire. On Tuesday, the House of Bishops approved him.[11]

When Harvard University was founded, its motto was "Veritas Christo et Ecclesiae" "which means the truth for

Christ and the church." Its crest showed three books, one faced down to show the limitation of human knowledge. However, in recent decades that book has been turned face up to represent the unlimited capacity of the human mind. In addition, the motto has been changed to one word, "Veritas," or truth.[12] The quest for knowledge is something we all should strive for; however, learning can cause us to lose insight of our limitations and latitude.

Knowledge and wisdom are two great possessions to have, but when you get so smart you cannot differentiate, distinguish, and rationalize the common things in life, you in essence have lost your sense.

Unfortunately, this is the state of contemporary society. As previously mentioned, America resembles Rome of yesteryear. Rome under its Caesars—Gaius, Caligula, Nero, and Domitian—was a military powerhouse of the ancient world. Rome's military was unprecedented, her garrison proficient, and her theaters and amphitheaters were breathtaking.

The fact that it was the first ancient city to have extensive paved roads brought truth to the saying, "All roads lead to Rome." Despite its pomp and pageantry, tapestry, tinsel, and ostentation, it still had an Achilles' heel. Rome crumbled just like so many other great civilizations. Why does this happen? Moral failure often serves as the foreboding wind that precedes military failure.

As we examine the first chapter of Romans, God gives us the answer for life's perplexing questions. There are some passages of biblical truths that are very pleasant, while there are others that are not. The truths we will discuss in this chapter are truths that are shunned by those consumed with a perverse lifestyle.

Before we dive head first into this chapter it is important that you recognize that whether you are straight, crooked, or gay, everyone is responsible for his or her actions. One reason why DL brothers remain in the talons of a DL lifestyle is that they blame it on being born that way. Claiming this defect is one of the excuses DL brothers use to help justify their lifestyle. When many come to this conclusion, they no longer fight the good fight against their perverse feelings.

It is essential for every person to recognize that he or she is either rewarded or punished for his or her decision. To live a gay, homosexual, or a DL lifestyle is a decision that you chose. To think that God does not hold us responsible for our actions is not only a demonic trick, it is a guaranteed first class ticket to hell.

Warped beliefs will certainly bring definite destruction. Although God made man a free moral agent, man is still judged by the decisions he makes. The very first glimpse we see of this is in Genesis 2:17. God told Adam that he could eat freely of all of the trees in the Garden of Eden with the exception of the Tree of Knowledge of Good and Evil. God told Adam that the day he ate of the tree, he would surely die. Notice that God didn't station a pit bull or a rottweiler around the tree to keep Adam and Eve away from the fruit, He simply said to Adam, "...the day you eat of the tree you will surely die." Up until the time that Adam and Eve ate of the tree, they were mortal people who possessed eternal life. They could have lived forever in their physical state.

Unfortunately, as soon as they ate of the tree, they were just as dead as dead can be. Adam and Eve's disobedience changed the course of their destiny. Why do you think they got kicked out of the Garden? They made the wrong decision. As a DL brother, if you think that you are not responsible for your actions, you are sadly mistaken. Maybe no one told you but you are responsible for your actions.

If you are not responsible for your behavior, I guess no one else is responsible for his or her actions or behavior either. The pedophile and the pervert who has a fetish for having sex with little children is not responsible when he molests children. This means the guy who rapes women, because he has a desire to have intercourse with every pretty woman he sees, once he's caught and arrested, should be released on the grounds that he was not responsible for his actions.

While we are listing people, let us not forget about the kleptomaniac. The reason why he steals everything that is not nailed down is that he was born like that. Therefore, the criminal justice system should clear up his rap sheet. Every man, woman, boy, and girl is responsible for himself. To think that you can do whatever you want, whenever you want, without being judged or confronted with consequences, you are sadly mistaken.

Chapter 1 of the book of Romans addresses the plight of a poisoned humanity. All of the major doctrines pertaining to the Christian faith—justification, sanctification, regeneration, and redemption—can be found in the book of Romans. As Paul wrote to the Christians in Rome, he wrote to help them understand how God expected them to live their lives.

If a man is to live a righteous life, he must first be apprised of what God desires of him. Once you know better, prayerfully, you will do better. The problem with many contemporary churches is they often substitute the interpretation of Scripture for the application of Scripture. Whenever the interpretation is inaccurate, the application becomes irrelevant. As Paul lays out God's intent for the Christian life, it is important to know that when God spoke His Word, He spoke with one thought in mind. In chapter 1, Paul addresses moral depravity. This depravity can be classified into four categories. The first category Paul addresses is a "Myriad of Impurities." This can be found in Romans 1:18: *For the wrath of God is revealed from*

*heaven against all ungodliness and unrighteousness of men who
hold the truth in unrighteousness...*

As you examine this passage, Paul makes it clear that it is
impossible for a person to hold truth in unrighteousness.
Those who attempt to hold truth in unrighteousness, the Word
of God states, to this person the wrath of God will be revealed.
Here, Paul describes those who are consumed with a Myriad of
Impurities. They are people who desire to overthrow God's
order, oppose the obvious, and ordain the obscene.

In the book of Genesis, God said that a man must leave his
mother and father, cleave to his wife, and they two shall become
one flesh. Whenever you do not line up with what God has
established, you will always have a makeshift relationship. Two
men who hook up together with the intent of getting married
are a classic example of overthrowing God's desire while oppos-
ing the obvious and ordaining that which is obscene.

Even if two men attempt to play husband and wife, they
must borrow from that which God ordained in order to do so.
A spouse is a husband or a wife. If you have two men together,
the question that comes to mind is who will play the role of the
woman (wife)? Someone has to play the role of the woman.
Since the role of husband and wife can never be filled by two
men or two women, people with an affinity for this lifestyle
have to play act or conjure makeshift relationships. Amazingly,
the people who reject what God has ordained, if they are to
play house, can't do it without borrowing from what God has
already established.

Let us take it a step further. If two men or two women
decide to adopt a child, they still must borrow from what God
created in order to do so. In order for a child to be in a union,
there must first be procreation. Since two men or two women
do not have the necessary plumbing to procreate, every time
they attempt to adopt a child they are forced to acknowledge

that which God has ordained. If you adopt a child, keep in mind that that child came as the result of a man and a woman. Therefore, the more you try to get away from God, you have to come back to God.

After Paul addressed a Myriad of Impurities, he secondly deals with a "Mind of Idolatry." Romans 1:21-23 reads, *Because when they knew God, they glorified him not as God neither were thankful, but became vain in their imagination, and their foolish hearts were darkened. Professing themselves to be wise, they became fools. They change the glory of the incorruptible God into the image made like corruptible man, and birds and four footed beasts and creeping things.*

A Mind of Idolatry involves a memory that is retarded, moral rebellion, and a Messianic replacement. When the Bible states in verse 21 how those who knew God refused to glorify Him, it is conveying the thought that there are some things God made that are relatively obvious. In Psalm 19, the Bible speaks of general revelation of God. This means that if you have never picked up a Bible, your common sense would still conclude by just examining the things around you that there must be a God. The fact that God strategically has the sun 93,000,000 miles away from the earth is evidence that God exists. Just suppose God would have placed the earth 92,000,000 miles away from the sun, we would burn up. Had He placed the earth 94,000,000 miles away from the sun, we would freeze to death. The same God who established the solar system is the same God who is responsible for the social system.

The actions of our contemporary society give evidence that a Mind of Idolatry has permeated our society. We are seeing more and more evidence of retarded memories and moral rebellion. Whenever man votes on what God wrote, it becomes obvious that his intent is corrupt. How dare dust make a ruling on divinity. How dare the creature make a ruling on the Creator?

Verse 21 states that *"when they knew him as God they refused to glorify him as God."* Any time you can change God, or change what God said, you reduce the veracity and the validity of God's Word.

In verses 24-26 Paul addresses a "Malignant Indictment." This involves a loving God, a lusting heart, and a lying man. Verse 24 reads, *Wherefore God gave them up unto uncleanness through the lust of their own hearts to dishonor their own bodies between them...* God is stating that He is going to snatch His presence from those who reject His Word so they can do whatever their imaginations deem. God is actually saying that He will allow them to do whatever they want.

What type of parent would allow his child to do whatever that child demanded? The reason we give them chores, curfews, and even ground them is because we love them. Keep in mind that every time a child is left to himself, dire consequences are involved. Good parents don't leave children to do what they please and then reward them for breaking rules. God does not sit by idly and allow us to do what we desire without suffering consequences.

Unfortunately, we have people who are now redefining God in a way that the Bible does not define Him. Have you ever heard someone say, "If God is so loving, why does He allow... to happen? Or, "God would never condemn anyone to hell because...."

It is impossible to come to know the God of the Bible without studying the Bible. Many people would rather trust the opinion and notions of people as opposed to God's Word. If you read the Word of God, you will discover that God is not only a God of love, He is also a God of judgment and justice.

As long as people circumvent how the Scripture defines God, they can make God into whatever they decide.

Anyone who does not approve of gay priests, gay bishops, lesbian lovers, DL brothers, or gay churches is often viewed as being homophobic. The aforementioned people, who are often religious, yet lost, often set their hat on the argument that God loves everybody and this is just a way of life like everything else.

Although God loves everyone, I think that it is important to clear up some murky waters. As the Bible reveals to humanity a loving God, it is important for humanity to know that the operation of God's love differs from the knowledge of just recognizing that God is love. Although His love may operate without conditions, it operates with restrictions.

In other words, there are guidelines according to love. Keep in mind that God's love for humanity is unconditional. There is not a thing that a person can do that will stop God from loving him. The problem with many people that live alternative lifestyles is that they get confused on the actions of God's love. John 3:16 gives us more than a glimpse of God's love, it reveals the extent of God's love. However, whenever we cross the bounds of what God forbids us from doing, God loves us so much that He chastises us. The Scriptures say that whom the Lord loves, He chastises. The chastisement of God is not placing us in a time-out. Rather it means that God determines a remedy or the rod of correction He deems necessary to bring His child back into subjection.

All through the Old Testament we are given vivid lessons about God's rod of correction. The Old Testament is placarded with picture after picture of how God chastised His chosen people. You can read from Genesis to Revelation and never will you find where God placed the nation of Israel or Judah in a time-out. Through the period of Judges, Kings, and

Chronicles, God chose to chastise His children often times by using their enemy as the rod of correction. When you read the book of Habakkuk, you will discover the reason why the prophet was taken aback by how the Lord chose to punish the nation of Judah. When God told Habakkuk that He was going to use the Babylonians to chastise Judah, the prophet could not believe it. Since God is sovereign, He can do whatever He wants, whenever He wants, wherever He wants and to whomever He wants. When you cross the metes and bounds of His commandments, you, like everyone else, will suffer the consequences of your actions.

I have been married for over eighteen years to one woman. I love my wife dearly just as she loves me the same. Our love for each other is unfeigned and unconditional. As unfeigned and unconditional as our love might be, within that love, there are some restrictions. It is because of the love that we have for each other that she and I recognize that neither of us has a license to do whatever we desire.

Whether you believe it or not, restrictions accompany love. Although I have the keys to every door in my house and every car in my driveway, I make it my business to be home by a decent time; the same holds true for her. These rules both written and unwritten were established for the betterment of the family because we love each other.

Keep in mind that regardless of what has been established, I can do whatever I want to do. However, when I choose to do whatever I want to do, I must suffer the consequences of my choices. If I stay out all night, live a riotous life, and just make it in before the sun comes up, although my wife might still love me, our relationship will, no doubt, become strained.

Love does not equate to stupidity. How dare I treat my wife any type of way, run over her feelings, disregard her desires and expect everything to be fine at home. If riotous living offends us, can you imagine how it offends God? God loves us so much that when we do wrong, He corrects us. According to the Scripture, when we do not accept the correction, we are bastards.

Another reason we are getting what we are getting is man's lusting heart. *Therefore God also gave them up to uncleanness, in the lusts of their hearts, to dishonor their bodies among themselves, who exchanged the truth of God for the lie, and worshiped and served the creature rather than the Creator, who is blessed forever. Amen* (Romans 1:24-25).

A faction in the Anglican Church is telling God, "The hell with you!" Why do men exchange the truth of God? They do not like what God has ordained. Any time you blatantly disregard the mandate of the Almighty, it is as though you point your puny finger in His face and say, "The hell with you."

The final thing Paul addresses is the "Infliction of a Malediction." Passions of desire, perverse dishonor, and prefabricated directions result in the Infliction of a Malediction. A malediction is a curse. Verse 26 reads, *For this cause God gave them up to vile affections…* There are not many places in Scripture where you hear God giving someone up, but this is one of those cases. As you read verse 26, notice who God is giving up or turning over. Keep in mind, He is addressing those with inordinate lifestyles. Also, notice what God is turning the person with inordinate affections over to. God does not turn them over to that which is good, holy, or sacred. He does not turn them over to a time-out teacher. The Scripture states that *God gave them up to vile affections, For even their women did exchange the natural use for that which is against nature.*

Can you imagine a boy who is pitted on smoking crack and his father looks over his shoulder and says, "Son, keep up the good work." Can you imagine a parent consenting to allow his or her child to become a prostitute? No parent in his or her right mind would sit by idly and watch a child waste away without at least attempting to divert them to the correct path.

Romans 1:26 is so clear, you would really have to strain to make this verse say something else other than what it is saying. Verse 27 reads, *And likewise also the men leaving the natural use of the women, burn in their lust one toward another, men with men, working that which is unseemingly. And receiving in themselves the recompense of their error.* Verse 28 reads, *Even as they did not like to retain God in their knowledge, God gave them over to a reprobate mind, to those things which are not seemingly.*

Kenneth Wuest talks about what it means to have a "reprobate mind," *adokimon noun.* The definition stems from the fact that the human race put God on trial (*dokimazo*), and because it rejected Him after trial, God gives it a "trial less" mind, one incapable of discharging functions of a mind with respect to the things of salvation.[13]

When God gives them up or turns them over, He gives them a mind that is actually no mind at all. They are at the point where their minds can no longer discern right and wrong; that capability is lost.

The Exposure Factor

Whether you believe it or not, we are all influenced by something. Children who love various sports such as golf, football, field hockey or tennis, in most cases, developed a love for their favorite sport because of their exposure to the sport. Oftentimes the degree of love that a child has for a sport is determined by the degree of exposure.

In the movie *Remember the Titans,* the daughter of Bill Yoast, the head coach, possessed knowledge beyond her years about the game of football. Her love for the gridiron was unmatched by most little girls her age. How did this young girl become so knowledgeable about football? Better yet, what was it that caused her to have such a love for the game? Did her understanding of football come as a result of osmosis? Did it happen because she had an intelligence that was above kids her age?

The reason little Sheryl Yoast had such a great comprehension and love for the Xs and Os was based on the fact that she was introduced to the game at an early age. Once introduced, she became indoctrinated and enmeshed in the game. As small as she was, Sheryl was more than a spectator; she was a cheerleader, a defensive coordinator, a head coach, as well as a fan. Chances are, she never would have become so engaged in the sport had there not been a strong presence of football in her home.

It was more than the introduction and exposure to football that piqued her interest. The town she lived in was consumed with football. It is one thing when a person lives in a football home but it is another thing when a person lives in a football town. Little Sheryl was indoctrinated in the gridiron. As a matter of fact, the game made such an impact on her that she had a greater preference for the pigskin than for doll babies and barrettes.

It is one thing to have a daughter that loves football but it is another thing to have a husband, brother, or a son who loves men. A proverbial phrase states that a "host of knowledge brings a host of sorrow." In essence, the more you know about some things, the more you don't want to know.

Just because a person is exposed to something doesn't necessarily mean that that person will fall head over heels in the new revelation. However, if the thing they have been exposed to gets a grip on them, it will often take an act of congress to emancipate them, especially if the thing they are exposed to gives them a rush.

First exposures make an indelible impression. Every drug dealer remembers his first run, every murderer his first victim, every crack head his first high, and every DL man his first encounter.

Just the other day, a TV news anchor was arrested for allegedly offering an undercover cop money for performing a sex act. What is it that would make a man jeopardize his job, lose his respect, and destroy his reputation? His feelings were exploited by what he had been exposed to.

One of the ways you deal with the Down Low is to make sure you limit your exposure to the clandestine lifestyle. When I suggest that you limit your exposure, I'm speaking in terms of absolute prohibition and not some passive periodic indulgence in some secret sinful society.

Since association fosters assimilation, one must be on guard so that he doesn't become a by-product of a bad environment. Kids who use racial epithets usually grow up to be adults that use racial epithets, because they are products of their environment. It is important that every DL brother knows that once you expose your feelings to the ways, patterns, and secrets of the DL, your feelings are prone to exploitation because of your exposure. For those who struggle with their sexuality, the more you are exposed to the DL lifestyle, the greater your risk of becoming consumed by it.

When I became a pastor, I made it a point to never counsel a woman without a member of my staff being a few feet away. I didn't do this because I was paranoid or because I thought that some unsuspecting woman, once the door of my office was closed, would jump across the desk into my arms.

My reason for having my staff an earshot away was to reduce and eliminate the chances of the wrong thing happening. See, I recognize that given the wrong scenario or circumstance, I, just like anyone else, am prone to fall. It doesn't matter how holy you are, or how holy you think you are, just like anyone else, you can fall.

It has been said that the man that does not think he can fall, is more apt to fall, while the man that knows he can fall is less apt to fall. The reason I take certain precautions as a pastor is so I can limit my liabilities. A liability is something that is a burden and not a blessing or a benefit; it debits your account rather than credits it, and in addition it takes away from you as opposed to adding to you.

The more you expose yourself to the DL, the more you increase your chances of becoming a liability to yourself and the people around you. Whenever you limit your liabilities, you better your chances in life.

If a child grows up in a good environment there is not a guarantee that that child will be a good child, but the odds are certainly in his favor that he would fare better than the child raised in a bad environment.

It was apparent why the news anchor was in the park the day he got arrested. He wasn't there to eat lunch, picnic, play in the sandbox or get a breath of fresh air. He was there because he knew that was the place where sexual favors were done.

Exposure can create such an insatiable desire within a person that it will render them void of rhyme and reason.

Notice how the right exposure can be good, while the wrong exposure can be bad. Some people have had their lives enhanced greatly because of early exposure to certain things. Kids who learn to read at early ages usually see how their reading skills help them in their later years. However, children who are exposed to sex at early ages are often faced with many hindrances: the hindrance of teen pregnancy, out-of-wedlock babies, STDs, commitment based on sex, and a host of other things that serve as crippling culprits to a young mind. Early exposure to some things can be likened unto attempting to take a drink of water from a fire hydrant; it will blow your head off.

There is a difference between being exposed to something and being involved with something. Many young boys and girls have been "turned out" or "tricked out" all because they were exposed to some freak show or introduced to some freak act by some perverted mind.

It is not an accident that kiddy porn is a multimillion dollar enterprise. When a child has been exploited as a kid, if that child does not get the help he or she so desperately needs, chances are they will be exploited again or exploit someone else.

Kiddy porn is a feeder into adult porn. Once this occurs, a damnable and destructible cycle is birthed. Oftentimes when those who have lived under oppression are emancipated from their enslavement, they in return oppress others. The same goes for the exploited. In many instances, the exploited becomes an exploiter. This is what the industry of porn calls residual value.

There was a reason why many cigarette or tobacco companies, for years, targeted children and teens in their advertisements. It was said that at one time that Joe Camel, on the Camel cigarette pack, was one of the most popular animated characters among young people. Keep in mind, the earlier a person is addicted to something, the harder it becomes to break that addiction. Younger minds are more malleable than older ones. As a young mind grows old, the addiction grows with it.

Pimps and prostitutes have a twisted relationship between them. The prostitute sells her body to make money for the pimp. Some prostitutes sleep with seven or eight men a day so that they can make their pimp happy. In lieu of painting every prostitute with a broad brush, I recognize that there are some women that are working in the world's oldest profession not by choice, but because they have been exploited.

As opposed to these women, there are other women who willfully allow their bodies to be exploited because they bought into a twisted deception. The twisted deception causes the prostitute to believe that prostitution is a legitimate and justified way of life. They long to please their pimp. They long for the day that they can make enough money to retire. They do what they do because they have been convinced or they have convinced themselves that their pimp really cares for them. Do you hear how crazy this sounds?

If a brother is to be delivered from the DL lifestyle he must do two things. First, he must change the way that he thinks. Second, he must guard his mind against things that cause him to act out of his God-made character.

Many African-American men are being pimped by the spirit of the DL. They are exposing themselves in public restrooms, soliciting strange men in parks, creeping around in areas where respectable people dare to tread, all because the spirit of the DL says, "I gotta have it!"

How do you overcome this demon? Guard what you expose your mind to. You will be surprised at the difference in your life when you take the necessary precautions to take yourself out of certain equations, change the company that you keep, and keep your mind renewed with the things that are righteous and true.

Keep in mind that association fosters assimilation. As a pastor, I make a concerted effort to hang around people with the same morals and values that I have. My reason for doing this is so that the people around me can balance me out. When I think of doing something crazy, thank God for friends who will balance me out, and vice-versa. When there is no one to balance you out, you will stay out of balance.

Where There Is Smoke,
There Is Fire

Have you ever heard of colloquial expressions such as "Where there is smoke there is fire;" "When it rains it pours;" "If it looks like a duck, sounds like a duck, walks like a duck; chances are, it is a duck." Many of you who are reading this book, especially women, are no doubt concerned about how to detect a DL brother. For the sake of a lengthy explanation, I would like to say that there is no foolproof way of knowing whether a person is homosexual, lesbian or on the DL.

Lets be real for a moment; every day we are conned and fooled. How many times have you read a newspaper study, or seen on TV, about people who today live normal lives but are actually fugitives of the law. Have you heard of people who have killed their entire family and moved to a different part of the country to begin a new life? After relocating, they remarry, unite with a church, become a Sunday school teacher, and are endeared by their community. What about the guy who was a mass murderer but is now the president of the Little League Association? What about the preacher who is endeared by his church, community, city, and country? Nevertheless, behind the wall of his accolades, there stands only a silhouette of truth and a fountain of fiction. Just as no good deed should go unrewarded, no unjust deed will go unpunished.

To a DL brother, life is about the good outweighing the bad. In other words, if your list of good deeds overshadows your list of bad deeds, your bad deeds are washed away by all the good you have done. Ideally, this may work to appease the DL brother's conscience, but it rarely works on the woman that he is involved with or married to.

Can you imagine the wife of a DL brother saying, "Although my husband and I have faced difficult situations just like any other relationship, overlooking the fact that he sleeps with a few guys, our good times together definitely outweigh the bad." How ridiculous can you get? Life is not about seeing whether your good deeds outweigh your bad ones. However, life is about respect, decency, courtesy, truth, and honesty. Life is about doing unto others as you would have them do to you.

One of the battles that African-Americans have had to fight constantly is racism. Racism is prejudice, bigotry, intolerance, and discrimination all wrapped in one. As bad as racism is, African-Americans detest something worse. It is hidden racism. One of the worst forms of racism is hidden racism. Although African-Americans detest racist people, the hidden racist is the vilest of the vile.

When you are confronted with a known, up front, open racist, you know what you are dealing with. You also know what to expect. The truth of the matter, when dealing with a racist who is honest and open about his or her convictions, you are generally never surprised about their actions. If ever there is a time that you are surprised, it is when they go against the grain of their own beliefs.

What makes hidden racism so bad is the fact that you never see it coming. It is like a cloak and dagger experience. You were set up. Someone lowered the proverbial boom on you. What makes it so devastating is the fact that you were unprepared. When you know you are dealing with a racist, you brace yourself or prepare yourself for all surprises.

With an up front racist, you brace yourself for the worst and settle for anything that seems good. However, with hidden racism, you never see it coming. You never expect it. Its bolo punch of deceit and deception will catch you with your guard down. To find out that you did not get the job or the promotion because you were judged on the color of your skin and not the content of your character and credentials is enough to make you livid.

Just about every African-American child is taught life lesson 101, which states you have to be twice as good as other folks in order to compete in life. Despite knowing this as we live the game of life, it still hurts every time we are confronted with racism. However, the hurt is magnified when we are at the receiving end of hidden racism.

A story is told of a man who stumbled on a snake that had been frozen. The man, out of the kindness of his heart, decided to be a Good Samaritan. With a heart of compassion, the man picked the snake up, placed him in his bosom and took the snake to his home.

After the snake defrosted, the snake bit the man. Shocked, angry and confused, the man asked the snake, "After all I did for you, how could you turn around and bite me?" The snake responded by saying, "You knew I was a snake when you picked me up."

Regardless of how people attempt to portray snakes as friendly and as good pets, they are still considered cunning, unlikable, dangerous, and deceptive. Regardless of what type of category you place a snake in—grass, garden, poisonous, or non-poisonous—to most people, a snake is still a snake. The same goes for those who live a DL lifestyle. Regardless of what type of spin you place on the DL to make it look good, it is a lifestyle that is cunning, unlikable, dangerous, and deceptive.

The DL lifestyle carries with it the fear of a snake and the devastation of hidden racism. Women who receive DL brothers into their bosoms, with the intent of being loved, cherished, and honored by them, are no doubt devastated when their DL man's clandestine life is revealed. Most women are not willing to share their man with another woman. If the truth be told, if their man is unfaithful to them they would rather it be with another woman as opposed to a man.

It doesn't make a difference what type of spin a DL brother places on his lifestyle, women will still classify his actions as being the lowest of the low. Garden snakes, grass snakes, poisonous snakes, and non-poisonous snakes are all snakes. Whether you, as a married man, sleep with a few men a year or only one man a year, classifying yourself as straight does not make you straight.

Gold is gold regardless of where you find it. The truth is the truth at ten o'clock as well as twelve o'clock. Infidelity, deceit, distrust and lies are the same despite how well you camouflage it as something else. DL brothers are not only destroying women, they are devastating them. The emotional, physical, and psychological damage that this lifestyle brings on women is more than most can bear.

There are a couple of reasons why the DL is not readily detected. As a pastor, I do a lot of marriage and pre-marital counseling. One of the sessions that I have couples in pre-marital counseling participate in is "taking off the mask." Taking off the mask is designed to get couples to be honest with each other. I discovered after years of counseling that most couples enter into relationships without being very honest about their feelings or some of the apprehension they have about each other. More times than less, the apprehension they have about their relationship prior to the consummation of their marriage will surface after the consummation of their marriage.

I know couples, both young and old, who suffer from an ideology that love conquers all. This theory may work in the cinema but not in real life. Listen friend, you cannot love problems away, you have to lovingly confront, address, and work through problems. If you have a child who cannot read, loving him will not help him to read. Although loving him will not aid in his reading, Hooked on Phonics® might.

My taking-off-the-mask session forces couples to address real life situations. As simple as this session is, I am constantly amazed by the profound results it brings. I commission both parties to go home and write on a sheet of paper five things that each would like to see changed about their mate. They are to write at least five things down on a legal pad. They are not to discuss any item on their list until they come back to my office. I am always amazed at the before and after results of this session. Usually, prior to this session couples tell me how they really cannot think of anything they would desire to see different in their mate. This is before I challenge them to write something down. After they go home and think about what I have commissioned them to do, I am always amazed at what shows up on their list.

How is it that in their first visit to my office everything was perfect, but on the next visit they discovered all sorts of things about each other that they would like to see changed. The truth of the matter is that they did not leave my office, go, and make up a list of concerns; the list was already made. The couples, for whatever reason, chose not to discuss or address their list of concerns because they usually think that either time or love will solve, alleviate, or eradicate problems.

The question of the day is, "How do you detect a DL brother?" To answer that question, let's start with some of the basics. Regardless of whether a man is on the DL or not, women must learn to take off the mask. Since there is a shortage of available black men due to prison, gang-banging, homosexuality, AIDS, etc., black women have to condition themselves not to have a "hard up" attitude.

In all honesty, it is not my intent to paint every African-American woman with a broad brush, but I have counseled many women who were more than willing to look past the obvious in lieu of dealing with the truth. I have talked to women who knew that their husbands were having extra-marital affairs before the affairs were exposed.

When I questioned them further and asked them how they knew their spouse was cheating on them, some of the responses I have received ran the gamut. I heard answers such as," they just knew," or "they had a feeling he was cheating," or, "they put two and two together," or "the Lord spoke to them." In many cases Romeo was actually Phoneo, but sister chose to overlook the obvious traits.

The first reason the DL is not detected is that women choose to look past things that are obvious. We all have something called intuition. Although this gift is attributed largely to women, men also possess the trait of peaking through hidden things that were never intended to be revealed. But intuition is an intrinsic part of every woman's makeup. If I had a dollar for every time my wife was right about her intuition, I could build a bridge to the moon.

Just because a guy attends church, dresses well, speaks the King's English, and looks macho, this doesn't constitute him being a man. Ladies, if you are trying to determine whether your man is on the DL, the first thing you need to do is to watch out for certain traits. Take a line from the straight guy script. Although straight guys never talk about it, they have a series of first-line defense tests to determine whether a brother is homosexual or heterosexual.

Straight guys determine whether a guy is gay by a myriad of things. If a guy walks, talks, looks, laughs, or acts feminine, he might fit the bill. Keep in mind for the sake of stereotyping people, I'm just telling you the way straight guys think. If he sings his words rather than says his words, rolls his eyes or sucks his teeth, switches when he walks, places his hands on his hips in reverse or is a mama's boy, he might fit the bill. If he has an affinity for many feminine things, like receiving flowers, if he likes watching promiscuous flicks involving orgies, etc., he may fit the bill. All of the aforementioned traits may help determine whether a guy is homosexual or on the DL.

The second reason the DL is not detected is that you don't really know the person. Over the past fifteen years that I have counseled, I am still utterly amazed at the number of people that come to my office for marital or pre-marital counseling who really don't know each other. People, by the droves, are getting hitched to people that they don't have a clue about.

I have often said that I would rather do a funeral or grief counseling as opposed to pre-marital counseling. Don't get me wrong, I don't have some type of twisted fetish or affinity for things that are morbid or involve mourning. The reason I prefer the mourner over the married is based on the fact that with the mourner you get his undivided attention.

When the mourner makes an appointment to see me, he is earnest in his quest. The mourner has no hidden agenda, no preconceived notions, and no point to prove. All he wants is guidance, wisdom and direction so he can move on with his life. However, the rascal that comes in for marriage or pre-marital counseling is a different cookie altogether.

Many of the people who come to my pre-marital counseling sessions are more interested in the planning of their wedding than they are their marriage. I believe that when there is clarity in the beginning there will be clarity in the end. If I had a dollar for every time some cool and debonair brother told his soon-to-be wife, "There is no need for counseling," or "I don't need another man to tell me how to handle my business," I would be rich.

Then there are the countless others who come to the counseling session knowing everything. The know-it-alls are the people who have nothing to say and nothing to add to the conversation because everything is fine and all is well. They want you to say your spiel so they can do their thing.

I am always admonishing couples to remember that what you see is what you get. It is my responsibility, as a man of the cloth, to lay all of the proverbial cards on the table, and that's exactly what I do. It is my responsibility to get both parties to look past the fantasy of thinking they can live off wedding cake alone.

I not only encourage them, but I charge them to learn as much about each other as possible. I ask questions such as, "How does he treat his mother? Do you know who his friends are? Has he shared the result of his latest physical? Do you know what type of credit he has? Does he pay his bills on time? Has he ever been arrested? Does he have any children? Does he take care of them? Is he saved? Does he attend church regularly? What type of church does he attend?"

My reason for asking some of these questions is to get women to think about the man that they are getting ready to marry. Ladies, regardless of how good your stuff may be, it ain't that good that it will change his character. Whatever he is doing prior to the marriage, I can almost guarantee he is going to do it after you marry him. The only difference is that the problem will most likely be compounded. All I am saying is do your homework. In the days and the times in which we live, women must learn to be Inspector Gadget.

Sometimes when I ask couples some of the pertinent aforementioned questions, if one or both parties begin to squirm, I know at that time that I have struck a chord. Keep in mind, you can tell a lot about a person by the company they keep. Just as water seeks its level, people do as well. I tell my children, all the time, that I hang around people that have the same morals and values that I have. This type of fellowship keeps me true to form.

Crooks hang with crooks. Pedophiles hang with pedophiles. Single men hang with single men, married men with married men, and DL brothers hang out with DL brothers. Do you know the person or guys that your man is hanging out with?

The third and final way you can detect whether a brother is DL is to watch for the change in his behavior. Regardless of how good an actor a person is, even the best actors stumble over their lines from time to time. Whether your man is having an affair with another woman or a man, behavior change is always a general indication that something is wrong.

Mood swings, overcompensation in affection, sudden withdrawal, excessive arguments, constantly needing time alone, and a lack of desire to make love are all general traits of infidelity. Don't get me wrong, these are not conclusive traits in and of themselves, but more times than not, when infidelity does occur, one or more of these traits are usually present.

Things to be on guard for:

1. Mood swings.

Mood swings involve constant change in behavior. It can run the gamut from wanting you around to the point of wanting to be away from you. In many instances, there is no rhyme or reason for some of the actions you will experience. I have discovered from various counseling sessions that the person who is the culprit of the infidelity usually places the blame on his spouse for why he acts the way he acts.

2. Overcompensation

Overcompensation involves somewhat erratic behavior. I'm not talking about general surprises or occasional nice gestures. What I am talking about is the going overboard mindset. All of a sudden he becomes persistent and undaunted about doing things that you have wanted him to do for years. Things that he has talked against or was vehemently against, now all of a sudden out of the blue he is consumed with fulfilling not only that wish of yours but other wishes as well.

3. Sudden Withdrawal

Sudden withdrawal involves your man clamming up or freezing up at inopportune times.

Most of the people that I know that have spats usually have to have a cooling down period after their spats. They may clam or freeze up momentarily, nevertheless, keep in mind that it is momentarily. This is different from sudden withdrawals. Freezing up for no reason, making your spouse go through a labyrinth of 101 questions to find out what's wrong with you, and being a Dr. Jekyll and Mr. Hyde are all definite traits that reveal that something is drastically wrong.

4. Needing Time Alone.

We all need time alone. The truth of the matter is that both men and women need an out. Whether it's playing golf, shopping in the malls, going to the movie, catching a football game, or going to a concert, we all need an out. However, something is drastically wrong with a person who constantly needs time alone. If there is a constant need for time alone, maybe your mate should have stayed alone. No one in his or her right mind gets married for the express purpose of being alone. When your spouse is always looking for time away from you, maybe it is because he or she desires to be with someone else.

5. A Lack of Desire to Make Love.

In my fifteen years of counseling, I have yet to come across a man whose wife was more into making love then he was. Most of the red-blooded American men I have counseled, whether they were spiritual, carnal, educated, uneducated, blind, cripple or crazy have been more interested in making sure that the "Love Jones" is intact.

When a man is lacking affection for his mate, it is usually because something is medically, spiritually, or socially wrong. Whenever a married man will go weeks or even months without making love (except for extenuating circumstances) to his wife, infidelity is almost always present.

In conclusion, as I stated at the commencement of this chapter, there is no foolproof way, right off the bat, of knowing whether a man is a DL brother or not. Therefore, I suggest that all sisters do their homework. Take some serious time to get to know the brother you plan to hook up with. There is a colloquial saying, "Fools rush in where wise men dare to tread."

Don't be fooled by the car, the crib, or how he is cut; do your homework.

chapter
SEVEN

May the Force Be With You

A few years ago, a blockbuster move entitled *Star Wars* hit the big screen. This galactic saga was nothing more than a space-age story between good and evil. This brainchild of George Lucas was an epic that was centered on the life of a simple farm boy by the name of Luke Skywalker. Luke along with his sidekicks, Chewbacca, C-3PO, R2-D2, Han Solo, and Ben-Kenobi, brought their wits together to rescue the lovely Princess Leia from the talons of the evil Empire. A nemesis Luke would soon have to face was Darth Vader. Vader, formerly Anakin Skywalker (Luke's father) was the secondary commander of the evil Empire. Vader, a former Jedi Knight, was seduced into crossing over to the dark side many years earlier. After his crossover was completed, Vader changed, both in apparel and appearance. Veiled in black, the man who once fought for light became a tutor and general for evil. With

Palpatine (the emperor) as his leader, the *Death Star* as his vessel, Vader's quest for dark power increased.

In *Episode V: The Empire Strikes Back,* Luke and Vader met face to face. Vader attempted to convince Luke to join him on the dark side. Vader's appetite had grown in such an insatiable manner that he fixed his eyes on ruling the entire galaxy. If Luke would just cross over to the dark side, he and Vader could plan the coup d'etat that would bring a father and son monarchy to the Galactic Empire. To Vader's dismay, Luke rejected his offer.

Episode VI: The Return of the Jedi found the champions of both the good side and the dark side face to face again. This time Luke was brought before the emperor. The proposal to join ranks with the dark side was extended to Luke once again. However, this time when he refused to join, he felt the wrath of evil fall upon him. Luke was brought before Palaptine to duel Vader in a saber light duel. It was not until Vader threatened to bring Luke's sister (Leia) to the dark side that Luke took up his lightsaber and commenced to fight.

As Luke visualized the thought of his sister crossing into an abyss of evil, he lost it. With every bit of rage in him, Luke attempted to kill Vader. After bombarding Vader with a barrage of blows from his lightsaber, Luke recognized that both Vader's and the emperor's wishes were coming true; Luke was making the crossover to the dark side. When Luke came to himself and realized what was happening, he renounced the dark side and all it stood for.

When it became apparent that Luke's resiliency held up to the dark side, Palpatine decided to kill Luke. With lightning bolts and energy surges, Palpatine inflicted pain on Luke.

Twisting and bending, Luke's body was ravished with pain. Amazingly, as all of this was transpiring, Vader stood by and watched. In the process of observing his son's destruction before his very eyes, Vader chose to act.

Vader attacked Palpatine. He picked the emperor up and threw him down a shaft. Unfortunately, his contact with Palpatine caused him to become mortally wounded. As he lay dying, a true reunion took place between father and son. A crippled, unmasked, and unveiled Vader spent the last few moments of his life speaking with his son not as good against evil, but good to good.

Whenever a man crosses over to a DL life style, he is crossing over to the dark side. Darth Vader's original name was Anakin Skywalker. As a young man, the dark side had seduced him. Once Anakin crossed over to the dark side, he discovered a completely new world, a new way of life, and developed an insatiable appetite to commit evil. When Anakin crossed over, he was no longer in control of his life because the force of the dark side held the reins. I don't know which grip was greater, the grip that Vader had on the dark side or the grip the dark side had on Vader. The same holds true for DL men—the success in their struggle for deliverance often depends upon which grip is stronger: the grip they have on the DL or the grip that the DL has on them.

Having an evil thought does not necessarily make a person evil. Keep in mind that none of us can stop bad thoughts from entering into our mind. However, we can keep them from staying. Bad thoughts don't necessarily make a person evil, but acting upon the meditation of those thoughts will.

When a man allows the reins of his life to be controlled by the DL, he is out of control. He becomes a cyborg of sensual desires. Monogamy, love, friendship, trust, and confidence are all words that become foreign to his vocabulary. Fidelity serves as a silhouette of truth and a figment of his imagination. His life becomes more secretive as the day goes by because he is walking on the dark side.

Once the dark side controls a DL man, he will definitely see a change in his life. Unfortunately, the change is not for the better, the change is for the worse. When Anakin, the former Jedi Knight, crossed over to the dark side, his name changed to Vader. Vader was a shell of Anakin. When a brother crosses over to the DL, he becomes a shell and a shadow of what he was or rather what he projected himself to be.

The Force of the dark side forces the DL brother into a myriad of changes. His thought process, affections, conversation and demeanor are all affected by the change. Since battles are won and lost in the mind, it is no surprise that the mind is the first thing that the dark side attacks. The dark side does not primarily war for a man's eyes, hands, feet, or any other part of his anatomy. The dark side wars for the mind.

The dark side wars for the mind for one express purpose and that is to control the body. Once the mind becomes consumed with darkness, it will influence the body to do whatever it deems. Once the mind is under this dark hypnosis, it more readily accepts and believes what it has been told.

It has been said that in ancient warfare some of the most brutal dictators governed just as effectively psychologically as they did militarily. A strong psychological stance would often open the door for an easy military victory. If the reputation of the dictator or warrior preceded him, his soon-to-be conquered subject or vassal would surrender without a fight. Why? The people were psychologically defeated.

In chapter 13 of the book of Numbers, as the children of Israel were on the brink of entering into the Promised Land, Moses sent twelve spies to enter into Canaan to spy out the land. The spies were commissioned to bring back some of the enormous bounty of the land and in the process find the best passageway both in and out.

When the twelve spies returned and brought Moses their report, ten out of twelve spies submitted an evil report and only two spies submitted a good report. Caleb and Joshua were the two men who came back with a good report. Caleb confirmed that the land was exactly as Moses stated. Caleb was so encouraged by what he saw that he said to the leaders and the nation, "Let's go up at once and possess the land, for we are able to overcome it."

Despite Caleb's and Joshua's confidence and courage, it was the report of the remaining ten spies that the nation chose to believe. The spy majority told Moses and the nation that the land was filled with people of great stature. It was a land that was consumed with many inhabitants. Although this was true, Israel still had the ability to possess the land. The last verse of chapter 13 really crystallizes the fact that wars are won and lost in the mind. After seeing the sons of Anak, "...*we were in our own sight as grasshoppers...*" Once the people saw these descendants they were psychologically defeated.

What a low self-esteem statement, what a spirit of despair, what a travesty. Despite having confirmation from God that the land was theirs, they chose to meander in the wilderness. What prohibited Israel from entering into the Promised Land was the perspective they had of themselves. A two-week journey turned into a forty-year journey, all because Israel came up with all types of excuses for not marching into the land. Excuses such as the people are too big and we are too small justified their failure.

The dark side will change the thought process of a man. It will make him conjure up excuses pertaining to why he sleeps with men. Once these excuses are justified in his mind, they build a level of comfort and complacency, which render his common sense useless. Regardless of the obvious truth that God made man for woman and woman for man, a mind that is hijacked by the dark side will rape him of his identity and force him to fulfill the role of an imposter.

It is no revelation that the male and the female anatomy are distinctively different. Men not only have a greater muscle mass than women but they also possess the ability to increase greater muscle mass than females. Even though men are more physical than women, women are more emotional than men. Although both have similar and distinct body systems, it is the distinctiveness of their body systems that really sets them apart.

The digestive, urinary, respiratory, circulatory, and nervous systems of men and women generally work the same but the reproductive system is a completely different ball of wax. Although the female is responsible for carrying the offspring, the male is responsible for providing the life (sperm). The female is dependant on the male for fertilization, and the male is dependant upon the female for incubation. This occurs because both male and female have specialized reproductive organs. The male reproductive organs are the testes and the penis, while the female organs are the ovaries, the fallopian tubes, the uterus, and vagina. In order for life to perpetuate, both male and female reproductive systems are needed. Men produce sperm and women have eggs. The role of sperm is to fertilize female ova (eggs) in order to produce life.[14] Through this process the cycle of life continues.

Human beings do not come into existence by a stork showing up on the doorstep. Childbirth does not occur by happenstance or a coincidence. It is through the reproductive labyrinth that the Almighty has established the human race. A man needs a woman to procreate and vice-versa. The Bible states that man was fearfully and wonderfully made. God not only made man and woman dependant on each other for procreation, he fixed their reproductive body parts so that the process of procreation and their intimacy would be pleasurable and accommodate one another. Neither men nor women possess the ability to procreate without each other. In addition, their bodies were not made in a fashion to enjoy intimacy from the same sex. A man's rectum was not designed to be penetrated for sexual pleasures. The reason God made men and women with different plumbing was to make them dependent on each other for both procreation and sensual pleasure.

It is a natural tendency for a man to be stimulated by a woman and vice-versa. It is natural for girls to talk about the finest boy on the football team or at their school. It is normal for boys to talk about which babe they plan to take to the prom. However, when a guy has a desire to take a guy to the prom and when girls get aroused by girls these are vivid indications that the dark side is stalking a person's mind and emotion.

Eagles weren't made to cluck and meander around in chicken coups. Chickens do not possess the ability to fly above storms, glide on air currents and soar for great distances. Although both chickens and eagles have feathers, beaks, and wings, there is a great difference between a chicken and an eagle. The first is a bird of the air while the other is a bird of the barn. Just as it is uncharacteristic to see eagles cluck, it is equally uncharacteristic of a man to be intimate with another man.

Everyone's cells contain a blueprint for life. Within its nucleus are twenty-three pairs of chromosomes, each constructed from deoxyribonucleic acid (DNA). Sections of DNA, called genes, contain the coded instructions needed for a cell to build proteins. These proteins control growth and development of the organs that give the body its individual shape and form. A cell's twenty-three pairs of chromosomes contain an instruction set of some 30,000-50,000 pairs of genes.[15] One member of the gene pair is inherited from your mother and another from your father. Amid the development of all of these genes, there is no such thing as a gay gene or a DL gene. When a man engages in a DL lifestyle it is unbecoming to what God created him to be.

Constantly meditating upon thoughts from the dark side is a primary inclination that you are a potential crossover candidate. Acting upon those initial thoughts will make you an honorary member of the dark side. Constant or periodic engagement in the thoughts from the dark side will most certainly make you a full-fledged member. Once you become a full-fledged member, it becomes harder to fight the dark side.

When a man's mind gets further and further away from the truth, it becomes more difficult to hear or heed the Word of God. When this occurs you will not only find yourself lying about your lifestyle but you will justify your lifestyle. When this happens, you are not operating in the Force. The Force is the will of God. The Force is God's decision and destiny for your life. When a man does whatever he is big and bad enough to do, he will hasten his own demise.

Why did fanatics crash two jets into the Twin Towers on September 11, 2001? What was it that caused Timothy McVeigh to rent a truck, fill it with explosives, and kill hundreds of innocent people? What is it that causes suicide bombers or homicide bombers in Israel and Iraq to blow themselves up along with hundreds of innocent bystanders? The culprit responsible for these accidents is the same culprit responsible for men who cruise on the DL. The answer to these questions is a seared conscience. When a person's conscience becomes seared to the truth, he is left to frame his own truth. When a person's conscience becomes so seared that he operates by his own controls, wishes, and whims, he has developed his own perspective for life. God, through the mandate of His Word, has given us a road map for life. If you read it, study it, and become a doer of it and not just a hearer, it will transform your life.

> *Finally, brethren, whatever things are true, whatever things are noble, whatever things are just, whatever things are pure, whatever things are lovely, whatever things are of good report, if there is any virtue and if there is anything praiseworthy—meditate on these things. (Philippians 4:8)*

MAY THE FORCE BE WITH YOU!

chapter EIGHT

Deliverance from the Down Low

T he headline for the August 2004 edition of *Essence* magazine reads, "Do Black Men Still Want Us?" The headline addresses the ills and vices of the DL, which is growing exponentially among the African-American ranks. The article unveils some of the frustrations and anxieties that African-American women are faced with.

Now that we have turned the corner of a new millennium, we have come up with a new game plan of life. The African-American male, throughout history in America, has had a tough plight. It is said that in 1619 the first African was brought from the coast of Africa to the shore of America. He was a thing to be used, and not a person to be respected. From that time to the late 1900s, many black men were lynched, castrated, and humiliated. He had to live through the stereotype of being classified as three-fifths of a man. Minstrel shows were performed in order to mock his manhood, malign his dignity, and destroy his character. Whenever whites walked in his presence, he had to respond by saying, *yes sum boss* or either *no maam.*

The fact that blacks, in slavery days, were prohibited from reading and writing was indicative of the fact that they were not brought to America the beautiful to prosper. Rather, they were brought here so that others could prosper from their so-called ignorance and labor. When you look at the history of the African-American male, the deck has always been stacked against him. The deck didn't get stacked when he came to America; the deck was actually stacked before he got here.

If you review African-American history, you will discover that there has always been an attempt to break the spirit of the black man. This was apparent the very first day he left the shores of Africa. Keep in mind that when he left Africa and came to America, he didn't come here on a Carnival cruise liner. He was chained as an animal side by side with other men of captivity in the stern of slave ships. He ate, defecated, and slept in the same area. The only time he was brought to the surface or on deck was to allow him to exercise. Despite slave trappers, auction blocks, plantations, minstrel shows, and Klansmen, God gave him an indomitable spirit. What was it that enabled him to bear his burden in the heat of the day? What was it that kept him going when many people would have given up? What was it that caused the most oppressed man in America to make it through lynchings and church bombings? It was his faith in God.

During the days of Jim Crow, white and colored signs, and segregation, the African-American man was more unified than at any time in African-American history. His faith was not something that he wore on Sunday; his faith was an intricate part of every fiber of his being. Now, freedom has brought apathy. Although there still remains a struggle from without, the greater struggle that haunts him today is the struggle that he must confront within. Liberation, to a certain degree, has opened Pandora's Box to a labyrinth of lasciviousness and immorality. The contemporized African-American male is a profound contrast from the African-American male of forty years ago. The black man of today is materially wealthy and morally bankrupt, while the black man of yesteryear was materially bankrupt and morally wealthy.

In today's society, greed has become his god as opposed to the time when God was his God. Just the other day, many black folks got mad with Bill Cosby because he said that black folks must become more responsible for themselves. He stated we must stop degrading our women in videos and stop blaming white folks for all of our problems.

After he made his comments, there were many black people who asked for his head on a silver platter. Some even asked, "Who does he think he is?" Why is he airing our dirty laundry all over the place? Who died and made him boss? Instead of rallying behind the truth of his statement, there were many who were taken aback by the bluntness of his comments.

I have discovered that the truth is the truth regardless of where you find it. The truth is the truth at ten o'clock as well as twelve o'clock. If the truth were told, there have been a lot of things through our years of existence in America that were designed to bring about our destruction, humiliation, disenfranchisement, and oppression. However, none compare to what we are doing to ourselves. Today's problem doesn't stem from the presence of poverty, rather it stems from the loss of purpose. If the truth be told, we have always had to do much with little. Our purpose as a people is misguided. Coming to America has not only granted us a license to live, it has granted us a license to be licentious.

There was a time when certain crimes were committed you knew it was someone other than a black person that committed that crime. A perfect example of this was in 2002 when the DC sniper terrorized the Maryland and Washington DC area. One of the reasons the sniper kept eluding authorities was because no one expected the sniper to be a black man.

We have been known to *gangbang* and commit *drive-bys*, but being a sniper was something that was foreign to us up until 2002. Just as John Allen Muhammad and John Lee Malvo shocked the world in 2002, the DL brother has shocked the world in 2004. Black men are pushing the envelope to the extreme. The man, who built this country on his back, is telling the woman, that God has placed by his side, that he "could care less" about her and her feelings.

To be a DL brother, in plain and simple terms is to be a phony, a liar, a stage actor, a masquerader, and a deceiver. What happened to us during slave trading was an atrocity, but what we are doing to ourselves today is nothing less than genocide. How is it that black folks can easily call white folks racist, but cannot see that we are racist against our own people because of the wicked things we do.

Why did the woman on the cover of *Essence* magazine ask that question? She asked it because many of our black men are lost. Unfortunately, although we make up about 13 percent of the American population, we are leading the country when it comes to HIV/AIDS.

Why is it that we make up 13 percent of the American population but more than 60 percent of the prisons population? Why is it that the graduation rate of black men is the lowest of any group? According to Bill Maxwell, Times Staff Writer for *St. Petersburg Times*, published January 2, 2004, only 35 percent of black men who enrolled in NCAA Division I schools in 1996 graduated within six years.[16] According to

J.L. King, a professed Down Low brother, DL or bi-sexual men are infecting 75 percent of African-American women with HIV/AIDS?

We can't blame white folks for everything. Don't get me wrong, racism still exists. The good ole boy system is stronger than ever. Yes, there are white folks who can profess they love Jesus, and still use the "N" word. However, aside from all of that there are some things we must stop doing to ourselves. One of the reasons why we are getting what we are getting is because we have lost our faith in God.

As I conclude this chapter, is my desire to conclude it with help, hope, and healing. Throughout biblical antiquity, whenever a man spoke on behalf of God, that man was never at liberty to say what he desired. He was always under a mandate to say what God wanted him to say.

There are countless times throughout the Bible when we read that prior to judgment, God gave a warning. We also see that when God's people were in trouble, He would often bring about deliverance Himself. Seeing that we have discussed all of the detriment of the DL, I desire to leave you with deliverance from the DL.

The case study for this deliverance comes from Mark 9:14-29. As we examine the passage, in order to be homiletically and hermeneutically correct, it is essential that we give the proper interpretation of the passage before we begin to make application. To make an application without interpretation causes us to be exegetically unsound. One of the problems we have in contemporized Christianity is that too many people are using application for interpretation.

Although this passage explicitly addresses a boy who was possessed with an unclean spirit, the ingredients used to deliver a demoniac are applicable to those who are suffering from homosexuality, lesbianism or a DL lifestyle.

To summarize the passage, Jesus has just come off a mountain accompanied by His three closest disciples: Peter, James, and John. As He comes down the mountain, a fiasco is taking place. Once He gets to the foot of the mountain, Jesus notices that the nine disciples, who had been at the base of the mountain, have just attempted a failed exorcism.

A distraught father, who is believed to have been looking for Jesus, brings his son to Jesus' disciples since he could not find Jesus. As the disciples attempt to deliver the boy from the demon, instead of the boy getting better, the boy gets worse. The sick boy's father is taken aback.

We surmise that either the man asked the disciples to heal the boy or the disciples, not knowing when Jesus would return, asked the man to allow them to heal the child. Either way, nothing happened. In short, the disciples brought the boy to Jesus and He healed the child.

If you are to be delivered from the DL or healed from homosexuality and lesbianism, there are four steps or prerequisites that are involved in your deliverance. The first prerequisite is you must recognize that "**IT IS NOT NORMAL TO BE ABNORMAL.**"

As I read this passage of Scripture, I began to applaud this father. My reason for applauding him is based on the fact that he did not turn a deaf ear or put blinders on when he noticed that something was visibly wrong with his son. One of the problems in today's society is that we are afraid to speak up when something in wrong. Mark 9:17 is actually a stark contrast to Mark 1:21-27. In chapter one of the Gospel of Mark, a story is revealed about how Jesus rebuked a demon-possessed man who was in a synagogue where Jesus entered. It is believed that the people who were in the synagogue grew accustomed to the presence of the demon-possessed man. As you meditate on the passage, notice that Jesus does not address the possessed man first, rather the man addresses Jesus. In essence, the man was accustomed to talking out of turn and the people in the synagogue grew accustomed to hearing the man speak out of turn.

The reason the father in Mark 9 brought his son to Jesus is that he knew it was **not normal for his son to act abnormal**. In verse 17, as the man informed Jesus about the plight of his son, he told the Master that his boy was controlled by a dumb spirit. The word *dumb* in the Greek comes from the word *alalos* which means "silent or muted."[17]

In verse 18, the father gives Jesus detailed information pertaining to what the dumb spirit caused the boy to do. The father tells Jesus that whenever this spirit seizes the boy, he is out of control because the spirit tears the boy up—makes him foam at the mouth, and grind his teeth.

A DL lifestyle or spirit will tear you. It will tear you down the line between what is right and what is wrong. It will tear you between the truth and a lie. It will tear you between denial and deception. Gone unchecked, this lifestyle will control you and consume you to the point that even when you want to do right, you continue to do wrong.

The father tells Jesus that every time the boy is controlled by a fit, he becomes speechless. The dumb spirit actually mutes the boy so he can not tell his father what is wrong. Regardless of the boy's inability to talk during the spasm, the father knows something is wrong with his son without his son ever telling his father that something is wrong.

The reason God has me addressing this issue of the DL is because those who are DL, homosexual, and lesbian are often muted by the spirit that has seized them. The aforementioned spirits will mute your mind and your mouth to the point that it will rape you of normal feelings and affections for the opposite sex, while forcing you to accept inordinate and unnatural feelings.

Just as it was abnormal for this child to be torn, to foam at the mouth, and to grind his teeth, it is also abnormal for a man to have sensual affection for a man. It is abnormal for a man to wear women's clothes, walk like a woman, talk like a woman, and look like a woman. It is abnormal for a man to live behind a wall of lies by portraying he is something that he is not.

Regardless of who deems it normal, it is abnormal for a man to mislead a wife, misuse the feelings of his girlfriend, or misrepresent to his children that he is one thing, only for the world to discover that he is not. In all honesty, it is a really low down thing to be Down Low. **THE FIRST PREREQUSITE OF HEALING IS RECOGNIZING THAT IT IS NOT NORMAL TO BE ABNORMAL.**

As I challenge those of you who struggle with the DL lifestyle to turn your vices over to Jesus, I also challenge the church of the Lord Jesus Christ to be compassionate to those who are seeking help. For those of us who preach the Gospel, we must not only speak with conviction against this sin, but we must do it with a heart of compassion.

I know that there are some people in the church who are homophobic. Maybe you don't know it but the church is nothing more than a hospital. The church has to be a place where the homosexual, the lesbian, and the DL brother can come in and find ointment for their wounds.

If God can heal cancer and bring people back from the dead, then sure enough He can alter your life by changing and transforming who you are. Remember that is not **NORMAL TO BE ABNORMAL.**

The second prerequisite of healing is recognizing that "DELIVERANCE IS NOT WITHOUT DESIRE."

In verse 19 Jesus rebuked His disciples by telling them that they were faithless because they could not deliver the boy. As

Jesus gave this rebuke, He had just come off the mountain with Peter, James, and John.

As you read this passage it becomes relatively easy to surmise that the father actually was not looking for the disciples, he was looking for Jesus. The reason we can infer this is because every time we see Jesus and His disciples together, the masses were not seeking the disciples, they were usually seeking Jesus.

Since the father could not get to Jesus, he brings his boy to the next best thing, which is the disciple. I submit unto you, that for those of us who are saved, spirit-filled, and living for the Lord, we are often the closest thing to Jesus that some people can see.

It is our job and duty to make sure that we do our level best not to damage people further than they are presently hurt.

For those who are secure in the "Ark of Safety" you can't get so homophobic and afraid that you think when you sit next to a homosexual, their homosexuality is going to rub off on you. You can't get so lofted up that when a person is truly looking for deliverance you impede their deliverance process because of your phobic behavior. The church is a hospital. If your church is not open for patients, you have gone out of business.

Some people are so saved they stink. Just because a DL brother's vice is having flings with men, you must remember that everybody has some type of vice. Sin is sin regardless of where you find it.

Many years ago when a young girl got pregnant, the elders of the church would have the girl stand in front of the church and apologize for her transgression. After she apologized, she would then ask forgiveness from God and the congregation. I was a firm believer then and I am one now that if that young girl had to stand up and confess to the church, every deacon in the church should have come before that altar also. Every preacher, usher, choir member, as a matter of fact the entire church should have been before the altar. The Bible declares, "Ye without sin, cast the first stone." Just because the DL is not your vice, you have no grounds to be pious. Whether your vice is a Miami vice or a Jacksonville vice, a vice, is a vice, is a vice.

Notice in verse 21, Jesus asked the father, "How long has your boy been suffering from these conditions?" As we examine the question of Jesus and the answer of the father, we need to be mindful that **deliverance is never without desire.** For those who are truly seeking liberation from the DL, remember, deliverance can never be experienced as long as you stand on the crutches of excuses. What do you mean, preacher?

In order to be delivered you must throw away every crutch you have used down through the years to justify your affinity and affection for men. You must rid yourself from the crutch of "I remember feeling this way when I was seven years old." "If God didn't want me to be gay, he wouldn't have made me like this." "I was molested as a child." "Someone turned me on to porn at a young age." All of the aforementioned are crutches you must get rid of.

Although the boy had been suffering for a long time, his father still sought out deliverance. The fact that Dad was still in search of deliverance was indicative of the fact that **deliverance is not without desire.** Dad could have made excuses for his son, but he didn't. Too many parents see the direction in which their child is headed, but don't say anything. Proverbs 29:15 declares that a child left to himself will bring his mother shame. One reason our children succumb to homosexual tendencies is that they are being left to themselves.

THE THIRD PREREQUISTE OF HEALING IS TO RECOGNIZE THAT "PAST FAILURE CAN IMPEDE PRESENT FAITH."

As the father sought help for his son, he almost allowed his past failure to impede his present faith. The word to those who are faced with DL or homosexual desires is, "Just because you were not able to overcome DL, lesbian or homosexual tendencies in the past doesn't mean that there is no help available."

One of the dilemmas that some DL brothers face is the fact that they have tried to attend church and go through religious programs. Some have been prayed over, prayed under, and preyed on. Some have been slain in the spirit, brought to the altar and had hands laid on them, but nothing has changed.

I would like to encourage you and let you know that just because you have met impotent people and attended impotent places of worship, that is no indication that God is impotent. Verse 22 commences with the dad giving Jesus further instructions about what the dumb spirit does to his son. He said that the spasm the boy had been having throws him in the fire and into the water. When we read the B part of verse 22 we see that a foreboding wind of doubt impeded the man's once clear faith. After the father finished telling Jesus how the dumb spirit was responsible for making his child go into spasms, he then asked Jesus, "If you can do something, please have compassion."

Notice that there is a contrast between this man and the man in Mark 1:40-41. In Mark chapter 1, Jesus crossed the path of a man who had leprosy. The Word declares that the man beseeched Jesus to heal him. He said that he knew that Jesus could heal him. It was not a matter of *if* Jesus could grant healing, it was a matter of *would* Jesus grant the healing. In contrast, in Mark 9 the father asks, "If you can heal my boy, would you do it?"

THE FOURTH AND FINAL PREREQUISTE OF DELIV-
ERANCE IS "RECOGNIZING THAT WITH GOD ALL
THINGS ARE POSSIBLE."

In verse 22, the father laid a tough hypothesis on Jesus. The
father asked Jesus if He could heal his boy. In verse 23, Jesus
flips the script by saying that the "if" is not on me, rather the
"if" is on you. Sensing that Jesus had just rebuked him, the
father apologized and then asked Jesus to help him to overcome his unbelief.

Regardless of what you have been through previously,
God is using this book as a medium to help your unbelief.
Unfortunately, through the past failed attempts, you have
questioned the power of God. Not only have you questioned
the power of God, you question whether God can deliver
you. Perhaps the question mark has come because you have
had some impotent encounter with some of Jesus' impotent
followers.

In verse 25, we see that as the people gathered around,
Jesus rebuked the spirit in the boy and charged it to exit his life
and enter no more into him. Verse 26 states that after the
demonic spirit cried and convulsed him greatly, it came out of
him. Many of the people who were standing around thought
the boy was dead.

Whenever you are coming from under a demonic strong-
hold, Satan always does his greatest work when he is on his
way out. Many of you who have gotten married can testify
that, prior to your wedding, maybe a week or two before the
big day, it appeared that Satan resurrected all your old
boyfriends and girlfriends to look you up. In many cases, when
God is on the verge of great deliverance it is because we are on
the verge of great destruction.

When Jesus called the foul spirit out of the boy, the spirit
caused great havoc. The foul spirit didn't come out of the boy

without attempting to work on the boy one last time. This is how Satan keeps you in the DL lifestyle. He will tell you, "Let's have this last fling. Let's just go out to dinner one more time. Let's just go to Disney World or Universal Studios just once more. Let's go to the movies, the family reunion, the family picnic or to the park." Keep in mind, Satan does his greatest work when he is getting ready to come out.

Regardless of what type of vice that you have, God stands ready, willing, and able to deliver you from the talons of wickedness. The apostle Paul makes an awesome statement about the unfeigned ability of God in Ephesians 3:20. In that verse, Paul stated that God has the power to do exceedingly abundantly above all that you can ask or think and it is according to the power that works in you. Wow! What a powerful statement! What an awesome word of encouragement!

Paul states that the God of the Bible can do exceedingly, abundantly, above all that you can think or ask. In essence, the apostle is saying that there is no limit to His power. That's a mighty God! He went on to say that God does this according to the power that works in us. 1 John 4:4 states that greater is He that is within you, than he that is within the world. This means the Holy Spirit who lives within you is greater than every demonic influence that attempts to control you.

If Christ is your Savior and Lord, Paul is stating in Ephesians 3:20 that the exceeding, abundant power that God uses already dwells within us. If you have the resurrected power of Jesus in your life, although the power in you is dormant, you through Christ still have the power to dominate the problem.

Philippians 1:6 states that we can be confident of this very thing, "he who began a good work in you will perform it unto the day of Jesus Christ." Regardless of what type of vice you have, or had when you came to Jesus, if you allow Him to work in you, He will work those things out of you. Jesus never starts a work that He does not finish.

SEVEN STEPS TO HEALING

1. Surrender your life to Jesus *(Romans 10:17)*. *So then, faith comes by hearing, and hearing by the Word of God.* Once you hear the word of God and receive it in your heart, you must totally surrender your life to Jesus. This means you no longer live for you, as in times past. You now live for God.

2. Recognize God will forgive you of your sins *(1 John 1:9)*. *If we confess our sins, he is faithful and just to forgive us our sins and cleanse us from all unrighteousness.* Keep in mind that sin is usually accompanied by guilt. If you sincerely ask God to forgive you according to this Scripture, He will. If God will forgive you, you should remember to forgive yourself.

3. Meditate on the Word daily *(Joshua 1:8)*. *This Book of the Law shall not depart from your mouth, but you shall meditate in it day and night, that you may observe to do according to all that is written in it. For then you will make your way prosperous, and then you will have good success.* This means it is imperative that you read the Word of God every single day. The first twenty minutes of the day should be dedicated to prayer and the reading of Scripture. You can start with reading one chapter from the Old Testament and one from the New. I would recommend an NIV or Amplified version. When you finish reading, pray throughout the day that God will grant you the wisdom and protection to do His will.

4. Have faith that God will change you *(Hebrews 11:6)*. *But without faith it is impossible to please God; he that comes to God must believe that he is, and that he is a rewarder of*

him that diligently seek him. Believe, in faith, that God can change you.

5. Change your behavior *(Proverbs 23:7). For as a man thinks; so is he.* The reason you must change your behavior is based on the fact that the people who have the same type of behavior will seek you out. If you go to a place where only a handful of black folks are present with many white folks, if you are black, chances are you will eventually gravitate to your people. Vice-versa occurs for white folks. The reason the DL brother, homosexual, or lesbian person has to change their behavior is that when a homosexual, DL brother, or a lesbian hits the room that you are in, they send out radar.

   Therefore, you must watch the way you walk, talk and how you project yourself. It is important that you carry yourself in a manner that you are not easily identified as one who is struggling with this type of lifestyle.

6. Change your association *(2 Corinthians 6:14, 15).* We are not to be unequally yoked with unbelievers. Make sure you cut ties with old friends and acquaintances immediately.

7. Don't forsake the assembly *(Hebrews 10:25).* Attend a Bible preaching, Bible believing church on a regular basis.

A struggling man's prayer

Lord, since You desire to work on my inward parts, I come to You without fanfare or façade. Broken, struggling, yet hopeful, some have said that You have been hope in ages past and are help in years to come. The pressures of this life have pulled me so until I have often given in to my feelings when I know I should have fought on. Despite my feelings, from this day forward I will place my full affection on both You and Your Word.

With the help and aid of the Holy Spirit, I know that I am more than a conqueror. Lord, since You fearfully and wonderfully made me, I desire to live my life to Your glory. Since association brings assimilation, I will no longer bask in conversation or companionship that is detrimental to my manhood. I will no longer put myself in positions that will cause me to become susceptible to my feelings.

Lord, I will read Your Word daily, talk with You through prayer daily, and make the necessary changes in my life that will enable me to live my life according to Your divine order.

Sincerely Yours,

Your Creation

Notes

1. Christian, Margena, "Men on the Down Low," *Jet Magazine*, May 3, 2004, Vol. 105, No. 18,32.

2. Warren Rick, *Purpose Driven Life* (Zondervan, 2002), 18.

3. *Webster's New World Dictionary and Thesaurus*, Second Edition, (Hungry Minds, Inc., 2002), 20.

4. Ibid

5. Wuest, Kenneth, *Wuest's Word Studies in the Greek New Testament, Volume I* (Wm B Eerdmans Publishing Company, 1955), 37.

6. Zoll, Rachel, *The Washington Times*, August 4, 2003.

7. Wuest, Kenneth, *Wuest's Word Studies in the Greek New Testament, Volume II* (Wm B Eerdmans Publishing Company, 1954), 125.

8. Wuest, Kenneth, *Wuest's Word Studies in the Greek New Testament, Volume II* (Wm B Eerdmans Publishing Company, 1954), 126.

9. Paul S. Taylor, "What's So New About the New Testament?", *Christian Answers Network* (ChristianAnswers.Net: As downloaded on December 12, 2004), URL: ChristianAnswers.Net/q-eden/edn-t022.html.

10. KFVS12 Viewpoint with Mike Smythe, 8/6/03 – Harvey Milk High School Copyright 2001-2003, KFVS12.

11. Zoll, Rachel, *The Washington Times*, August 4, 2003

12. Grounds, Vernon C., *Our Daily Bread, A Selection of Daily Devotional Readings from the Popular Devotional* (Discovery House Publishers, 1997), 320.

13. Wuest, Kenneth, *Wuest's Word Studies in the Greek New Testament, Volume I* (Wm B Eerdmans Publishing Company, 1955), 37.

14. Walker, Richard, *Encyclopedia of the Human Body* (DK Publishing, Inc., 2002), 212.

15. Walker, Richard, *Encyclopedia of the Human Body* (DK Publishing, Inc., 2002), 247.

16. Maxwell, Bill, *St. Petersburg Times*, January 2, 2004.

17. Wuest, Kenneth, *Wuest's Word Studies in the Greek New Testament, Volume I* (Wm B Eerdmans Publishing Company, 1955), 181.

Deliverance from the Down Low
Order Form

Postal orders: Mymax Corporation
P.O. Box 58104
Jacksonville, FL 32241-8104

Telephone orders: (888) 504-7151

Web orders: www.deliverancefromthedownlow.com

Please send *Deliverance from the Down Low* to:

Name: _____

Address: _____

City: _____ State: _____

Zip: _____

Telephone: (_____) _____

Book Price: $12.99

Shipping: 1-2 books $3.82
3-5 books $4.54
6-8 books $5.80
9-11 books $6.42
12 books and over $7.85
7% sales tax applies to Florida residents

Or order from:
ACW Press
1200 HWY 231 South #273
Ozark, AL 36360

(800) 931-BOOK

or contact your local bookstore